Intimacy

Kaleidoscope

Statement of Purpose

Kaleidoscope is a series of adult educational resources developed for the ecumenical church by Lancaster Theological Seminary and the United Church Board for Homeland Ministries. Developed for adults who want serious study and dialogue on contemporary issues of Christian faith and life, Kaleidoscope offers elective resources designed to provide new knowledge and new understanding for persons who seek personal growth and a deeper sense of social responsibility in their lives.

Kaleidoscope utilizes the expertise of professionals in various disciplines to develop study resources in both print and video. The series also provides tools to help persons develop skills in studying, reflecting, inquiring critically, and exploring avenues of appropriate Christian responses in life.

Kaleidoscope provides sound and tested resources in theology, biblical studies, ethics, and other related subjects that link personal growth and social responsibility to life situations in which adult Christian persons develop.

Intimacy

The Quest for Life Connections

James W. Hanna

Combined Leader's Guide and
Student Edition

A Kaleidoscope Series Resource

United Church Press
Cleveland, Ohio

KALEIDOSCOPE SERIES

United Church Press, Cleveland, Ohio 44115
© 1992 by United Church Press

Biblical quotations and adaptations, unless otherwise noted, are from the New Revised Standard Version of the Bible, © 1989 by the Division of Christian Education of the National Council of the Churches of Christ in the U.S.A., and are used by permission

All rights reserved. Published 1992

Printed in the United States of America
The paper used in this publication is acid free and meets the minimum requirements of American National Standard for Information Sciences-Permanence of Paper for Printed Library Materials, ANSI Z39.48-1984

97 96 95 94 93 92   5 4 3 2 1

Library of Congress Cataloging-in-Publication Data

Hanna, James W. (James William), 1940–
    Intimacy : the quest for life connections / James W. Hanna.
       p. cm. — (A Kaleidoscope series resource ; 2)
    Includes bibliographical references.
    ISBN 0-8298-0889-2 (alk. paper)
    1. Intimacy (Psychology)—Religious Aspects—Christianity. 2. Christian life—1960– I. Title. II. Series.
BV4597.53.I55H36 1992
248.8'44–dc20   92-34045
                                                                              CIP

To Becky,
my intimate partner,
and
our children,
Anita, Lisa, David, and Mark

*Even if I cannot see you, if I cannot touch you,
I feel that you are with me.*
                              Gabriel Marcel

Contents

Introduction to the Kaleidoscope Series — xi
How to Use the Kaleidoscope Series — xiii
Preface — xv
Acknowledgments — xvii

1. Search for Intimacy — 1
2. Fearful Intimacy — 21
3. Escapes from Intimacy — 41
4. Expressions of Intimacy — 59
5. Making Life Connections — 77
6. Building Communities of Personal Support — 97

Notes — 117

Selected Bibliography — 125

Leader's Guide — 127

Introduction to the Kaleidoscope Series

Through direct experience, our faculty at Lancaster Theological Seminary discovered that a continual demand exists for Christian theological reflection upon issues of current interest. To meet this demand, the Seminary for many years has offered courses for lay people. To offer the substance of these courses to the wider Christian public is the purpose of the Kaleidoscope Series.

Lancaster Seminary exists to proclaim the gospel of Jesus Christ for the sake of the church and the world. In addition to preparing men and women for the ordained Christian ministry, the Seminary seeks to be a center of theological reflection for clergy and laity. Continuing education and leadership development for all Christians focus our mission. The topics and educational style in the Kaleidoscope Series extend Lancaster Seminary's commitment: theological study reflective of Christians' interaction of the Bible, the world, the church, worship, and personal faith. We hope that this course will provide an opportunity for you to grow in self-understanding, in knowledge of other people and God's creation, and in the spirit of Christ.

We wish to thank the staff of the Division of Education and Publication of the United Church Board for Homeland Ministries for their support in this enterprise. The Rev. Dr. Ansley Coe Throckmorton, The Rev. Dr. Larry E. Kalp, and The Rev. Dr. Percel O. Alston provided encouragement and support for the project. In particular, we are grateful for the inspiration of Percel Alston, who was a trustee of Lancaster Seminary. His life-long interest in adult education makes it most appropriate that this series be dedicated to him. Two other staff members have guided the series through the writing and production stages: The Rev. Willard Wetzel, Project Coordinator for the Kaleidoscope Series, and The Rev. Nancy G. Wright, Editor for Kaleidoscope. As a publishing staff they have provided valuable experience and counsel. Finally, I wish to recognize the creative leadership of Jean Vieth, the Seminary Coordinator for the Series, who has been active for several years in this educational program at Lancaster.

Peter M. Schmiechen, President
Lancaster Theological Seminary

How to Use the Kaleidoscope Series

The Kaleidoscope book is the basic resource for all students in the Kaleidoscope Series. In each Kaleidoscope book there is a Leader's Guide bound into the back of the book. The leader will need to study both the text and the Leader's Guide to prepare to lead study sessions of the Kaleidoscope Series resources. The accompanying video is a very helpful tool for the class using this book as a study resource.

Other KALEIDOSCOPE resources are

- BREAD FOR THE BANQUET: *Experiencing Life in the Spirit*, by Elaine M. Ward
- THE GIFT AND THE PROMISE: *Becoming What We Are in Christ*, by Peter Schmiechen
- GOD, WHERE ARE YOU? *Suffering and Faith*, by Richard F. Vieth
- NOBODY'S CHILD: *A Generation Caught in the Middle*, by Paul E. Irion
- STRETCH OUT YOUR HAND: *Exploring Healing Prayer*, by Tilda Norberg and Robert D. Webber
- THUNDER ON THE RIGHT: *Understanding Conservative Christianity*, by Elizabeth C. Nordbeck
- JOURNEY THROUGH THE PSALMS: *A Path to Wholeness*, by Denise Dombrowski Hopkins
- BECOMING PEOPLE OF THE WAY: *Intentional Christianity*, by Francis Ringer
- PASS IT ON: *Telling and Hearing Stories from John*, by Gilbert L. Bartholomew

Preface

Although this book began as a continuing education event at Lancaster Theological Seminary, the human experiences that fill its pages are primarily taken from my background as a pastor and my practice as a therapist presently directing a pastoral counseling center.

The quest for intimate connections is universal, of course. But those who have the courage to confront their own inner demons and angels in therapy chart for the rest of us the struggle involved in the search for intimacy. I admire their courage more than I can say.

Those who have participated in my workshops and retreats on intimacy have become my companions on this journey. Their questions and challenges have clarified my thinking. I once thought intimacy was simply a dimension of human relationships. I now know that although human interaction provides our primary model for understanding intimacy, it is only part of the universal truth that we are created for intimacy with all life.

Acknowledgments

When I agreed to write book, I asked Karen Carnabucci to assist. Karen is familiar with my thoughts on intimacy, having attended my workshops and interviewed me extensively for newspaper articles; and she appreciates the context out of which these ideas have been formed. She has been a newspaper editor for sixteen years, writing on family life and relationship issues. She is presently a therapist with Caron Family Services, where she works with patients with addictive, codependency, and intimacy concerns. Working with her has been a pleasure. She has added clarity and substance to my ideas and to the book.

Chapter One

Search for Intimacy

Intimacy [is] the wish to know another's inner life along with the ability to share one's own.
                                                    Lillian Rubin

Three Vignettes

Tom and Theresa sit in the counselor's office, their bodies turned slightly away from each other. They have been married for thirteen years, but on this day they avoid making eye contact. Their eyes shift to the floor, to their hands, to every place except to each other.

They are attractive people, and they are informed and articulate, as their college educations and professionals jobs suggest. They have two healthy children. Tom's income has allowed Theresa to put her career on hold and voluntarily stay at home to care for the family. But today, they are speaking of divorce, a word that was for them unthinkable on their wedding day thirteen years ago.

Theresa complains that Tom is not supportive at home, and she wants him to spend more time with the children. She also is afraid that Tom will leave her. She knows other women her age, neighbors and former co-workers, who have been abandoned by restless husbands. Tom responds to the situation by withdrawing emotionally, saying he feels restricted by her demands. But he also feels immobilized by what he describes as a moral obligation to stay in his marriage.

* * * * * * *

Laura has already weathered two marriages, the first to an irresponsible man who abandoned her with three small children, the second to an alcoholic who was emotionally unstable. Through determination and hard work, Laura sought child care after her second divorce and climbed from part-time menial jobs to a middle-management career that has offered financial security.

She has been less successful in establishing a lasting relationship with a man. Although she has found new friends at a singles' group in her community and has begun to feel comfortable with her "singleness," dating has been sporadic and disappointing.

Laura says the men she likes rarely call after the second date, and those who call aren't the men she likes. She questions her ability to enter into and maintain a relationship with a man. She says she knows so many interesting women in her age-group and wonders why she can't find men who are equally compatible. She feels vulnerable and fearful of being hurt again, and yet she dreams of finding a companion in her life.

* * * * * * * *

Sheila is known throughout her neighborhood as a busy housewife who finds time to make casseroles to welcome new families to the block. She remembers birthdays and anniversaries of friends, former classmates, and her husband's co-workers with gifts, cookies, and cards. She frequently takes in neighbors' children on Friday evenings after the parents casually mention that they haven't found a baby-sitter.

When Darlene moved into the neighborhood, Sheila responded with invitations to bring Darlene's daughter Linda to Sheila's house to play with her own two children. Sometimes the two women would have coffee together, and sometimes Sheila would encourage her new friend to catch up on her shopping while she looked after Linda. Sheila believed that they were developing a friendship based on mutual interests, and soon Linda became a daily visitor to Sheila's home. But when the situation changed Sheila told Darlene that she could no longer care for Linda after school. Now Sheila feels confused because the relationship has cooled considerably. When she meets Darlene in the supermarket aisle, their conversation is perfunctory and stilted.

In each of these three situations, as different as they appear, we see the common human quest for intimacy, the experience of feeling connected in important ways to another person. Although this urge for connection finds its most immediate expression in relationships between people, which will be our primary focus in this book, the quest for intimacy points to our need for wholeness in all our relationships—with the created order, with ourselves, and with God.

Expanding Our View

It is important that we expand our view of where we experience intimacy in our lives. A committed marriage provides fertile ground for a lifelong journey of intimacy, but marriage is not the only setting for important personal relationships to develop. A community during a time of catastrophe, a group's fact-finding trip to a Third World country, or a weekend church retreat all become opportunities for intimate connections if we are open to them.

The case of Jessica McClure, the toddler from the small community of Midland, Texas, who was wedged in an abandoned well after a freak accident, illustrates connections forcefully. The highly publicized ordeal in October 1987 became the focus of concern of millions of people throughout the country. As rescue workers labored for fifty-eight hours to dig Jessica from the well, the residents of that small town, as well as television and newspaper reporters from metropolitan cities, became emotionally involved with Jessica's family and with each other. As it became apparent that the plucky little girl was alive, even then being lifted from darkness to light and was within the grasp of loving arms, those anxiously waiting reached out to each other, touching an arm, a hand. Men spontaneously hugged each other, several threw their arms up, celebrating and laughing.

This was an occasion of intimacy. The people of that rural community had come together with an urgent task, to rescue the toddler. But as they continued during the week to bind their hands, hearts, and minds to the rescue work, they transcended their personal interests and differences. They felt bonded in caring and concern, an experience so potent that even those people watching on television felt moved.

At such a time, we identify with the distressed family, the struggling workers, and the innocent child. Their sufferings affect us and dissolve the barriers that often stand between us. For a moment, our inner eyes are opened, and we glimpse a spiritual reality of connection, just as real as the child, the workers, the family members, and the well that caused the accident.

In 1988, I joined a small group of "observers" to visit the war-torn Central American countries of Guatemala and Nicaragua. While in Nicaragua, we visited several villages where groups of peasants were building houses with the help of volunteers from Habitat for Humanity (an international organization that works in partnership with poverty-stricken people to construct homes). These modest homes were constructed from bricks and lumber produced from raw material gathered from the area. Most of the families in the villages had suffered the loss of a father, brother, or other male relative in the cruel fighting that consumed their land. They had no medicine and little food. Yet they did not meet us with despair. The villagers reflected hope for a better future, for a day when the war would end and they could grow their crops and live without the daily fear of attack.

In one community we assembled with a group of villagers in a small unfinished structure. The roof had blown away, and cold winds blew through the open windows. We stood there as strangers to each other, worlds apart in language, customs, and life experience. Just a week before, we were told, three of their villagers had been caught in a fatal cross-fire between Sandanistas and Contras. To gather information and to keep warm we stood shoulder to shoulder, talking through our translator. As our conversation concluded, one of the villagers was asked to pray. His voice was calm and assured. He obviously possessed a spiritual grace and inner poise beyond anything I had anticipated. My own prejudice about uneducated peasants was challenged. Without understanding his words, we visitors were lifted into a spiritual bond with the village people as he spoke. Later, our guide translated a portion of the prayer: "All the Christian groups in the world are praying for this country. They understand the pain and anguish we are suffering in our bodies here, but in the name of Jesus of Nazareth, we praise You. Put these people in Your arms of love and guard and protect them."

His prayer was an appeal for intimacy. In that moment, we were no longer observers; we were participants brought together in spite of our many differences, feeling a part of this community as we shared their hardships and their faith.

Intimacy can develop also in a temporary community, such as a weekend retreat. A dozen participants are gathered in a cozy room of a retreat center. A few sit cross-legged on the floor while others relax on the sofa, away from the center of conversation. Each has been asked by the workshop leader to recall an experience of intimacy, and one man begins to speak.

As Jerome talks about the progressive illness that has claimed the vitality of his wife, his eyes begin to fill with tears. He remembers how his wife's illness has depleted his own energy and zest for life. He talks of the prolonged hospitalization, which has not returned her to health, and of their early years together. He begins to sob as he recalls seeing a rare glimmer of life in his wife's usually blank eyes during hospital visits.

The others listen respectfully, empathizing with Jerome's loss and loneliness. But as he continues something more happens. A presence of attentiveness is created in which each person is connected with the humanity of the other. Without prompting, several group members comment on the closeness they feel.

In the process of becoming acquainted, each person takes the opportunity to speak while others in the group listen attentively in return. Then Jerome becomes comfortable enough to disclose to the others a painful aspect of his life. His honesty opens a door for the community, welcoming a new level of openness. Group members offer emotional support as they listen without interrupting or giving advice, and then become willing to share their own experiences, whether a comparable situation in their own lives or a feeling that was stirred as they heard Jerome's story.

Therapeutic communities for treating drug addicts, including alcoholics, understand and cultivate this potential for transformation through intimacy. First, the mood-altering substance is separated from the chemically dependent client. Then outside distractions are eliminated so that the addicts can focus on identifying and discussing the reality of the effects of addiction on them. As they peel away their denial that they are affected, patients touch base with their feelings and explore and mourn their many losses: self-esteem, financial security, family and friends, or a positive sense of self. As they repeatedly choose to share the secrets and humiliations of what they did to obtain their drug, and the pain of their addiction, they allow others to know them. They also reinforce in each other their commitment to abstain from the substances and activities that have enslaved them and, in this way, participate in their own resurrection. No longer are they people alone in their pain and weakened by circumstances. They have become recovering people with a network of support and with a new sense of identity, strength, and purpose.

Often people who participate in therapeutic communities—despite their differences in social background and economic status—find genuine intimacy as they explore their human struggles together. This is the reason that Alcoholics Anonymous and other twelve-step recovery groups that have branched from it have been successful. They bring together diverse groups of people who find healing and fellowship with one another. This is true despite the fact that there are no leaders, no advertising, and a pass-the-bucket budget.

We can be close to each other in many ways. We feel love for our friend as we watch a spectacular sunset or listen to music performed by a beautifully conducted symphony orchestra. What parent, coming home after work to see her child standing at the rail of his crib with a crooked smile of delight, does not feel her heart melt? We can feel deeply connected emotionally in the moment of recognition that we and another person are indeed friends or lovers. The theologian and philosopher Martin Buber viewed such intimate moments as I-Thou encounters. The other is no longer an it, an object to be analyzed and mastered, but a Thou, whose inner wholeness or essence is revealed. Such encounters cannot be devised or planned; they are not the result of our efforts. In Buber's words: "The *Thou* meets me through grace—it is not found by seeking."[1]

Yet there are ways in which we can open ourselves to the possibilities for intimacy in our world. In developing and strengthening our abilities to be self aware, to disclose ourselves, to listen empathetically, to affirm the presence of others, to be spontaneous and tolerant, we can create a context in which intimacy may occur, greatly deepening the life we share with others.

Toward a Definition of Intimacy

As I look closer at intimacy, I am reminded of the words of a friend. "The idea," he said, "is to have a great trip, not to read a map." The ideal intimacy is an experience, not a definition. The map is not the journey. Yet it's important to look at some of the characteristics that comprise intimacy in order to clarify the experience.

The word *intimacy* is derived from the Latin *intimus*, meaning "inner" or "innermost." To know the *intimus* of someone assumes a particular kind of understanding, a knowledge of the core, the inmost character of the person.[2] This kind of understanding goes beyond the intellect to an intuitive grasp of the inner reality of oneself and another. It is this emphasis on knowing the inner reality that supports a commonly held definition of intimacy as "the wish to know another's inner life along with the ability to share one's own."[3]

Such a definition infers an ability to be open, mutual and non-judgmental. Yet it also makes a significant assumption: the inner life is something defined and stable. In fact, it is continually changing. It changes because it contains feelings and perceptions, intentions and imaginings, questions and uncertainties about life. The way we understand ourselves has been strongly influenced by the messages and definitions we have heard and experienced from the significant people in our lives, particularly in our early years. All this invites us toward a process of growth and self-understanding. But before we look closely at this understanding about intimacy we carry from early years, we need to examine some of the popular images of intimacy.

Cultural Images of Intimacy

We all have our special pictures of intimacy, gleaned from a multitude of sources including movies, television, advertising, and popular music. We add these cultural images to our personal picture of intimacy that we have seen among family members and neighbors. We thus build a kind of scrapbook of how we think things should be between people.

In popular thinking, intimacy often appears as synonymous with sexual love. We speak of "intimate relationships" or an "intimate conversation," implying that intimacy has to do with private, confidential matters. As we will discuss later, while sexuality is certainly an expression of intimacy, not all sexual expression creates intimacy. An understanding of sexuality as the path to greater intimacy can be lost, however, on a soap opera mentality, which equates sexuality with genital activity and sexual technique.

In such a mentality, the sexual dimension of intimacy is exploited, and relationships lack permanence. When the thrill of romance fades, the relationship may end; if it does not, it may continue out of a sense of duty or obligation. Such physical relationships are seldom seen as occasions for partners to expand through difficulties to an appreciation of their personal differences. Nor are they often viewed as opportunities "to awaken and bring forth our finest human qualities, such as awareness, compassion, humor, wisdom, and fearless dedication to truth."[4]

One of the most common cultural images of intimacy is that of the mythical other, the perfect partner who will meet completely our emotional, spiritual, and sexual needs. This myth suggests that our placing the "right" person in our life is the key to making intimacy happen effortlessly and quickly. This search for the right "fit" is based in fantasies of romantic love, some stemming from thousand-year-old fairy tales supported by twentieth-century movies and popular songs. Advertising punctuates the "right person" message by suggesting that a particular toothpaste, pantyhose, or automobile will clear the way to deeply fulfilling romantic love.

Cultural images can create unrealistic expectations. These interfere with people forming deep connections with others and may encourage them to move from relationship to relationship in search of perfection. Rob, for example, had vowed not to repeat long-distance relationships that had meant exhausting travel and expensive telephone calls. So he became acquainted with Susan, a woman who lived and worked in his city. She was attractive and charming, and they enjoyed similar interests, including bicycling and the theater. As they began dating, Rob concluded that Susan would be a suitable marriage partner. She was educated and politically involved, as he was, and they shared the same religious background and interest in starting a family. He believed that he had found his "dream woman" after more than forty years of being single.

But as the dating reached the six-month mark, Susan went for outpatient surgery for a troubling knee injury. It was then that Rob discovered another side of his dream woman. Even though he sent Susan flowers after the operation and volunteered to shop for her while she was recuperating in her apartment, she became clingy. Rob felt that she accused him of being insensitive. Susan, on the other hand, felt that Rob dismissed her when when she tried to talk about her fears of aging and continuing health problems. Obviously, when she was ill and needy, Susan no longer met Rob's image of the perfect fit. And Susan discovered that when she was under duress and fear, when she showed a more vulnerable side of herself, Rob no longer lived up to the strong and caring image that she had admired.

Part of the challenge of intimacy is to accommodate the differences we discover in each other and to move through our disillusionment when our expectations of perfection confront the reality of another person's humanness. If Rob had been able to take time to listen for the feelings underlying Susan's complaints and had tried to understand her quite reasonable fears, he might not so quickly have labeled her actions and words as "childish" and "bitchy." If Susan had been able to reach out, to talk honestly to several other friends, she might not have pressured Rob to become her primary source of security at this fearful time. As it was, she had neglected her women friends because of her excitement about her relationship with Rob, and few of them knew of her health problems or surgery. If Rob and Susan had been aware of their own feelings and resources, and had taken risks to share them appropriately, each might have participated in moving the relationship to a deeper and more complex level. Instead, each partner's limitation became the focus of the other's disillusionment, and neither confronted personal narrow expectations of the other's behavior.

In the early stages of a relationship, the emphasis is often placed on areas of compatibility and similarity. Differences are minimized, ignored, or denied. Couples preparing for marriage will often present idealized pictures of each other and resist any effort to discuss areas of conflict. For example, when Bess and Paul, a couple in their twenties, were preparing for marriage, they were seen by their family and friends as an ideal couple. They did in fact share many common interests, and since they had started dating, three years prior to their engagement, they spent most of their time together. Paul was now completing his graduate study in chemical engineering; Bess was finishing her second year as an elementary school teacher. In time, however, their differences became apparent and undeniable. For example, during an argument, Paul would withdraw and sulk. When Bess would push for a resolution, Paul would blow up; then there would be more silence and frustration.

Even the qualities in the other that had been attractive became the focus of tension and conflict. Paul's laid back nature covered his passivity in dealing with problems; Bess's active, can-do attitude disguised her tendency to be controlling.

We popularly refer to such a situation as "the honeymoon is over." Yet it is only when the honeymoon is over that the real intimacy begins. With some help Paul and Bess were able to acknowledge their differences and accommodate them in dealing with conflict. Paul learned to state his views more openly, rather than withdrawing and arguing with Bess in his head. Bess learned to create space for Paul during conflict by containing some of her intense emotion and stating her needs less aggressively. It was only when they moved beyond holding tenaciously to the idealized image of each other and expanded the image to include the foreign parts of the other that intimacy occurred.

First cousin to the image of the perfect fit is the image of the ideal family. The television generation of *Leave It to Beaver* and *Ozzie and Harriet* and the more current and affluent Huxtables, created by comedian Bill Cosby, picture the way parents want their children to act. The little ones are obedient and endearing, cuddling up with picture books with a relaxed Mom and Dad, who are always at home when needed. The older children are enthusiastic and involved, and if they talk back to Mom and Dad, it's all in fun. Life's problems are solved in segments of thirty minutes, just in time for everybody to gather at the family table for the Norman Rockwell Thanksgiving, as the beaming matriarch brings out a platter of turkey to a waiting and grateful family.

Aspects of Intimacy

Tom and Theresa's Story: Distance and Closeness

Let's look again at Tom and Theresa whom we met at the beginning of the chapter. Our unhappy couple stand on the edge of divorce, yet yearn for a sense of family closeness. Theresa, the worried wife who fears that Tom will leave her, mirrors her mother's insecurities in her own marriage. At a young age while growing up, Theresa had become her mother's confidante. She heard her mother complain constantly about her hard-drinking husband's frequent absences. Theresa's own relationship with her father, a successful businessman, was built on fantasy rather than reality. He was often away from home so that Theresa knew very little about his thoughts, feelings, and dreams. When she met Tom, she was impressed by his decisive manner, strength, and professional success. She saw him as someone who would take care of her and listen to her.

Tom, it seems, has had much practice in listening to women. His mother regularly approached him with family problems, rather than discuss them with her husband. Problems, not feelings, were the focus of the home, and Tom became the family spokesman, since his siblings viewed him as the intermediary between them and their parents. These skills of negotiation have served him well in his managerial job, where his ability to talk calmly among a variety of viewpoints is admired. At home, however, he fears losing his independence so resists the childhood role of problem solver by distancing himself from Theresa and rarely shares what he thinks or feels.

Tom and Theresa do not know how childhood roles contribute to their feelings and perceptions today. Their unspoken beliefs that their past is in the past are keeping them from recognizing the unhealthy patterns that developed in their original families. Theresa does not understand how her mother's constant fears of abandonment infected her view of the marriage partnership. Nor does she recognize that she had no choice as a youngster in hearing adult concerns, concerns that should rightly have been shared with an adult friend or a professional therapist. Theresa also is unaware that she suppressed her own emotional needs as she listened to and comforted her mother and that she is still repressing them today. For instance, when she tells Tom she wants him to spend more time with the children, what she really wants is attention for herself.

Tom also does not recognize the involuntary role he played as family problem solver when growing up. As his father slowly abdicated his responsibilities at home, Tom's mother focused on her oldest son, using him as a sort of surrogate husband. Although Tom gained family respect in the decision-making role, he did not identify and discuss his own feelings about his mother's domination of his home life. His father, on the other hand, modeled the masculine role of the man who distances himself from his family rather than assert his individuality and express his feelings. Tom felt praise only when he attended to other people's needs.

Neither Tom nor Theresa is aware that both have suppressed anger because of the family dynamics that dictated they take adult responsibilities as youngsters. Much of the anger they feel is misplaced, so that they bring recriminations and defensiveness to each other in even the simplest of interchanges. The situation means that Tom and Theresa are alone together—without identifying the common background they share and their difficulty in asserting their needs directly. They cannot understand why their own family isn't feeling as good as it looks. They are angry and hurt, but mostly afraid. Their outward complaints hide their deeper fears of being abandoned or being engulfed.

Both of these fears—abandonment and engulfment—are expressed in many ways in their intimate relationships. At this point, it is important for us to acknowledge that such fears are not restricted to a few people; they are a part of us all. The particular way we work out these fears in our intimate relationships is a reenactment of our childhood role, but the urges to distance and to relate, to separate and to bond, for solitude and for community are a part of the universal human drama.[5] The intimacy dance involves a balancing of our need to be an "I" and our desire to be a "we."

Laura's Story: Power and Cooperation

If intimate relationships confront us with our need for distance and for closeness, they also present us with the necessity of balancing our need for power and for cooperation, for control and for surrender. At the deepest level of being, these polarities reflect two fundamental attitudes toward the mystery of life, which the psychiatrist Gerald May defines as willfulness and willingness.[6] These attitudes are not restricted to partner relationships only but are basic stances that people take in all aspects of life. Those who emphasize one side or the other are apparent. Willful persons maintain a tight control over themselves, their world, and others and are threatened by the unpredictable and unexpected; overly willing persons are compliant, always eager to please, and desire to put others' needs first.

In the ideal situation, we achieve a balance between love of ourselves as individuals and love of ourselves and others in communion. We live with a sense "I" that suggests personal intention, motivation, and determination, all important characteristics in making life choices and in taking a direction in our world. But we also live with a sense of "we" that suggests an opening to cooperation and compromise, an essential component in dealing with others.

Laura's story of unsuccessful marriages illustrates the pitfalls of leaning too far in one direction or the other. Laura, who grew up with a domineering and critical father, pledged to herself as a teenager that she would not repeat her mother's marriage choice. Because of her desire to remain in control of her life, she successively became involved with men who were weak and dependent, men she could easily dominate through caretaking and intimidation. In her first marriage, she took charge of making all the family's social plans for weekends and holidays, rarely consulting her husband, and she also paid all the bills and doled out an allowance to her husband. In her second marriage, she often threatened to leave her husband when he drank heavily and talked about telling his family about their financial problems.

Although these dependent men acquiesced to her decisions and threats, they were not emotionally available to Laura; they rarely asked her about her feelings or concerns. Nor did they directly share their anger with Laura about her take-charge behavior. They simply walked out when they could not tolerate it any longer. With such partners Laura felt independent and in control, but she also has continued in adult life to miss what she did not receive from her father—affection, emotional support, and a truthful exchange of feelings.

Compromise and surrender are threatening elements to Laura because in her mind they mean weakness. She is still trapped by her fear of domination by others, especially by men. When Laura feels drawn to a relationship that appears to have a balance of power, she pulls back. She finds an imperfection she says she cannot tolerate in a man. As she withdraws in fear of being hurt, she continues to remain alone. Again, the outward complaints hide deeper fears.

Laura has not learned to balance power and cooperation. This would be essential to her achieving and maintaining closeness with a marriage partner.

Sheila's Story: Giving and Receiving

Beyond distance and closeness, power and cooperation, intimate relationships also call for a balancing of a third dynamic, the need to give and to receive, specifically the need to give and receive affection.

Indeed, giving and receiving can be difficult for many people. For the under-affectionate person, any gesture of admiration is hard to accept, whether it be an expression of liking or affirmation, a material gift, or affection expressed physically or verbally. Because the under-affectionate have decided they are unlovable, they avoid close relationships, fearing that if others knew them they would surely reject them. Their response to their fear is to emotionally distance themselves from others, often by becoming extreme givers. They hold people at a distance by giving to them without receiving what the others have to give. But under-affectionate people can also distance themselves through behavior or words that offend or hurt others.

The overly affectionate person, on the other hand, seeks extreme emotional closeness with others, wants to please them, to be liked. Such people often demand the affection of others and interpret the need of others for space as a sign of their own rejection. They often are not only demanding receivers but controlling givers, holding others captive by their generosity and self-sacrifice.

The good neighbor Sheila illustrates the give-and-receive phenomenon. Neighborhood people often remark on Sheila's thoughtfulness, her attention to other people's celebrations and special occasions. But Sheila is slowly learning through her recent disappointment with Darlene that giving to someone doesn't guarantee the person's friendship and sometimes hinders it. She knows now that she wasn't saying what she wanted or needed from others but was giving material gifts, energy, and time so that others would need her and depend on her. As Sheila realizes that her need to "do" for others has historically overridden her need to take care of herself, she feels betrayed by the other families and individuals in her neighborhood who are not as grateful for her favors and gifts as she would like. But she also knows she betrays her inner needs when she says yes to others when she really feels like saying no. She has put aside her personal well-being, her goals and projects, to please others.

An important awareness came when her friend Darlene offered Sheila a set of metal lawn chairs her family no longer used. Sheila, who, remember, had often taken Darlene's child for baby-sitting, then offered Darlene an old bureau Darlene had admired. Sheila speaks ruefully about the exchange. It was an even exchange but has not drawn the two women closer. Their bond had been broken when a behavior problem with Darlene's daughter surfaced. Sheila told her friend that she could no longer offer regular child care because the problem was taking time away from her own children. The friendship then cooled considerably.

Sheila now sees that the exchange of goods and favors with Darlene was a substitute for true friendship. She expresses confusion about how the bond ended, and sadness and anger that the pair was unable to express what happened regarding the babysitting arrangement. They could not resolve the issues and keep the friendship intact. Sheila recognizes that she avoids people because her feelings are strong and that she doesn't always give herself permission to disclose her feelings.

Intimacy as Self-Disclosure

By now, it may be clear that self-disclosure is essential to intimacy. Self-disclosure means revealing our feelings, thoughts, and intentions. This is risky and so is intimacy. Intimate relationships unmask our hidden selves, and this unmasking may be painful as well as joyful. As we come in contact with others, we run the risk of being changed, of coming to experience ourselves differently than we had previously. Unless we are willing to face the unknown in ourselves and in others, we will not proceed far along the path toward intimacy. If we withdraw in the face of our feelings, whether fear, sadness, joy, or perhaps anger, then we limit the opportunities for being with others and for expanding our capacity for intimacy.

Although self-disclosure is essential to intimacy, in the interests of deeper intimacy there are times when it needs to be contained. John Welwood helps us understand the need for this process of containment when he says, "Impulsively expressing everything we feel or venting emotions because we are uncomfortable containing them will eventually overwhelm our partner, thereby constricting and shutting down communication.[7] To impulsively express anger, for example, cannot only overwhelm others, but can prevent us from understanding our own feelings or hurt or disappointment that may lie underneath.

Donald, for example, had no trouble expressing his anger. His temper would often explode with others, especially the employees in his small business. He would justify his expression of anger by saying that at least others knew where he stood. He prided himself on being "honest" with his feelings. Some of his employees who were intimidated by his anger kept their distance; others just did not take him seriously. But Donald was perhaps the person most affected negatively by his reliance on anger as his primary expressed feeling. He remained deprived of understanding his other feelings, such as hurt, fear, or disappointment underneath his anger, and because his anger became the focus of attention, others did not discern his humor and gentleness, other parts of his inner life.

Jordan and Margaret Paul in their very helpful book *Do I Have to Give Up Me to Be Loved by You?* make a distinction in conversations between responses intended for protections and those intended for learning.[8] The intention to protect gives rise to any defensive and self-justifying response in the face of a perceived threat; this response is motivated by fear. The intention to learn gives rise to a desire and commitment to explore and understand. Following this path of learning means becoming vulnerable and open to ourselves and to others. We try to explore, to understand the underlying reasons for our feelings and behavior, to move below the protective surface into the inner reality of ourselves. In doing this we also understand others. The path of intimacy leads us to a creative appreciation for this inner reality so that we seek ways for its expression.

Intimacy as Mutuality

When people come to psychotherapy, they often want answers. They will ask, "Why do I feel this way?" or "How should I handle this situation?" I often feel a temptation to respond to this immediate expectation, to relieve the tension, to provide solutions. Such responses, however, seldom help the persons and could abort a deeper understanding that is is essential to their growth. I think of the words of Rainer Maria Rilke, which I have posted above my desk:

> Be patient toward all that is unsolved in your heart and try to love the questions themselves like locked rooms or books that are written in a foreign tongue. The point is to live everything. Live the ques-

tions now. Perhaps you will then gradually, without noticing it, live your way some distant day into the answers.[9]

The questions are the gateway to understanding. We are seldom helped by other people's answers to our questions. Helping persons as a psychotherapist is partly the art of asking questions that challenge or expand the worldview of the other person. Insight given before the questions have been lived and addressed is useless and deprives the person of the opportunity to probe more deeply into his or her own answers.

There is no doubt that honoring the questions of others—without giving advice or help—can be difficult at times because it can be painful to watch another struggle with a situation we've already resolved personally. We may even feel the consequences of their unwise decisions or behaviors. Intimacy, however, is the art of living our questions in the presence of another and of being present with another in the living of their questions.

The quick proffering of help does not leave space for people to explore and question their own motivations, dreams, and needs. Mutuality means respecting the boundaries in our relating to others, creating space for them to struggle with their questions and decisions. Consider the case of Carolyn, who had been dating two young men since her high school years. She often spoke to her parents about which suitor would be best for her. Her parents favored one young man over the other and said she seemed happier and more lively when she was in his company. When she expressed questions about the relationship, they minimized her doubts and compared her experience to that of her older sister, now happily married.

Carolyn finally married the young man her parents liked, but during the first year of marriage, the couple experienced a great deal of financial difficulties that affected other problems between them. When Carolyn told her mother about her problems, her mother assured Carolyn that she was simply adjusting to married life. The parents then offered to lend the young couple a sizable sum of money to purchase a larger and more comfortable house in the suburbs.

Quick answers or partial solutions of this sort may foster dependence on the part of some recipients or stir rebellion in others As well-intentioned as quick answers may be, they do not allow people opportunity for exploring their own solutions, which is vital to any growth process. Such protective behavior in adults is often only a shelter for the younger generation and keeps them from struggling with their own daily living. However, protection can show up in many kinds of relationships, besides parent-child, where the parties are uncomfortable with ambiguity.

Alex is an uncle concerned about his nephew, twenty-year-old Rick, the son of his divorced sister. Rick attends a community college and brings home grades that are undistinguished. From his vantage point, Alex believes that Rick has no clear goals in life. He worries that the young man will forfeit a solid education that should be the stepping stone to a good job later in his life. He also recalls his own confusion at that age when he was experimenting with drugs. Alex wants to take his nephew aside and tell him it is time to begin to make important decisions regarding the future.

But telling would be easy and may have a negative reaction from Rick. It will be a genuine challenge for Alex to provide a loving male presence in his nephew's life without making pronouncements or judgments. He needs to help the young man to identify feelings and to voice questions about his goals, even as he affirms Rick's resources. One positive approach could be for Alex to share his own struggles at the same age, to talk about how some decisions are not easily made, and that plans made, even those he makes today as father of two small children, take time and thought to flesh out. By taking such a route, Alex would practice mutual respect, allowing Rick the dignity of making his own decisions.

Intimacy as Sustained Familiarity

Another aspect of *intimacy* is expressed in the Oxford Universal English Dictionary definition: "the experience of close, *sustained familiarity* with another's inner life" [italics added]. A romantic attraction between two people may occur when they first meet, but intimacy requires a sustained familiarity and mutual commitment. Sustained familiarity means coming to know the other over time, a process of peeling back the layers of what is obvious to get to the inner level of feelings, beliefs, and hopes. Commitment is the resolve to deal with the obstacles that inevitably arise in this process. Erik Erikson, the pioneering developmental psychologist, describes a part of intimacy as "the capacity to commit oneself to concrete affiliations and partnerships and to develop the ethical strength to abide by such commitments, even though they may call for significant sacrifice and compromise.[10]

This commitment can only come out of a determination to move beyond defensive behavior to more openness to oneself and to the other. It is not imposed from the outside but is an inner choice process that confronts the barriers to relating. It can be formally stated in a marriage vow or religious vow, or it may be assumed in a friendship. But whatever its form, commitment is an intention to persevere, to accommodate again and again to the changes and demands of relating to another person. As psychologists Evelyn and James Whitehead write: "A well-developed capacity for intimacy enables a person to honor the promises and demands of commitment and to sustain with integrity the adjustments and compromises required in living with others.[11]

To honor the promises and demands of commitment is not confined to a relationship to a significant other. It can also be expressed in our solidarity with the human struggles of others whose names we may not know but whose humanity we share, or in solidarity with the created world in which we live. Such commitments should not be made too lightly before we have had an opportunity to assess the cost. Taking the risk to share of ourselves, however slightly, gives us the chance to assess our view of ourselves and others. But the reward of such a journey is a growing communion with each other, with the world we live in, and with the Source of all life.

Chapter Two

Fearful Intimacy

Intimacy . . . is a way of being in which the tension between distance and closeness is dissolved and a new horizon appears. Intimacy is beyond fear.

Henri J. M. Nouwen

There is no fear in love, but perfect love casts out fear; for fear has to do with punishment, and whoever fears has not reached perfection in love.

1 John 4:18

Fear and Intimacy

"Fear is the great enemy of intimacy,"[1] writes the theologian Henri Nouwen. Yet intimacy also arouses fear. The fear that inevitably emerges in our search for intimacy can have many faces—the fear we may not find what we seek, the fear of being exposed, or the fear of rejection. Intimate relationships confront us with these and other fears, but in the words of psychologist John Welwood, "at the core of all fears of intimacy is a fear of loss."[2] We tend to fear either being left alone and abandoned—the loss of love—or being engulfed, emotionally controlled—the loss of self. Such fears are not academic or benign; they infiltrate the very fiber of our lives, causing us to act in bizarre ways at times. Our response to such fears can have many expressions, but generally we run from each other into "fearful distance" or cling to each other in "fearful closeness."[3] I suspect we each have a familiar tendency, either to run or to cling, yet each is a part of our lives at many levels.

Henri Nouwen points out that it is often in the social context that we can see these tendencies of fearful distance and fearful closeness most obviously expressed. For instance, we like to keep our homes a safe distance from prisons and mental hospitals, and city planners often bypass ghettos in building highways so that travelers are not offended or frightened. The well-known NIMBY principle (Not In My Back Yard) often emerges when a social service agency makes plans to organize a group home or outreach center for mentally retarded adults, battered women, AIDS patients, the homeless, or recovering drug addicts. Our social consciences know these are admirable enterprises, and we even may endorse them politically or support them financially. It is often difficult, however, to accept them when we imagine an ambulance pulling up weekly at the back door of a home for the elderly or looking into the blackened eyes of a battered woman with her frightened children in tow hurrying to the shelter across the street.

In conversation, we discuss safe topics or deal with safe issues.[4] The football game, the previous evening's television show, the busyness of our workday, all offer ways to interact with others without probing a person's feelings deeply, offending someone, or disclosing our own painful feelings. A hospice nurse I know has observed how friends and relatives of her terminally ill patients will often distance themselves physically or emotionally from the patient, especially when they learn the fatal diagnosis from the physician. If the friends and relatives do continue contact with their loved one, they may ignore any talk of physical or emotional pain or of the illness. The nurse sees visitors controlled by irrational fears, which deprive the ill person of needed nurturing and support.

While growing up in a small community in western Pennsylvania, I was part of a real-life scenario nearly identical to Harper Lee's classic story *To Kill a Mockingbird*. At about six years of age, I was instructed to avoid a certain house not far from where I lived. The fact that the house was located at the edge of town adjacent to a small wooded area only lent to the air of mystery. I concluded that a strange and dangerous person lived there, but the nature of the strangeness or of the danger I never discovered. I took the warning seriously because I knew that other children also skirted around the forbidden residence. As I recall the events, it is hard to know what, in fact, was said and what was the product of overactive childhood imaginations. But rumors spread that the mysterious person had guns and threatened children. It was only later I discovered the strange person was a retarded adult who was harmless. Most probably, the loneliness of his disability was compounded by a community that directed their children to evade him, that feared him. In the powerful *To Kill a Mockingbird*, which explores many aspects of fear and prejudice, the children eventually become curious about the mysterious Boo Radley and attempt to befriend him. But there are many communities where such people are evaded, ignored, and even ridiculed.

Such episodes of childhood intrigue are not uncommon. My childhood incident illustrates the universal tendency to project evil intentions on people who are different and to distance ourselves from that which we fear. It is this tendency to project and distance that can lead to what author and philosopher Sam Keen calls the "hostile imagination," the capacity to abstract and depersonalize, even invent, an enemy. According to Keen, the simple assumption behind the hostile imagination is that "what is strange and unknown is dangerous and intends us evil. The unknown is untrustworthy."[5] In *Faces of the Enemy* Keen powerfully and soberingly describes the thinking process that creates national enemies in order to justify and legitimize one country's violence against another. A part of this process is to dehumanize enemies, to distance by fearful imaginings from that in them which is human, which makes them like us. We invent names for enemies—calling them monsters, demons, infidels—accusing them of barbaric acts, madness, and immorality. By doing so, we deny that these people also fear death and suffering, have families, love children, hurt when wounded, and have dreams and doubts. Such a process of dehumanization is a prerequisite to "eliminating" the foe.[6] (Keen cautions that imagining evil and inventing enemies does not mean there are no real enemies.)

It is important that we be aware of the process of distancing that helps to create an enemy. We can become conscious of the same dynamic at work when we meet the unknown, the different, in any relationship, including in those we love.

On the other hand, we escape into safe closeness by creating structures such as cliques, groups, or clubs, "places where people huddle together in mutual admiration or common suspicion of the outsider."[7] Whether they are sororities or fraternities, country clubs or political parties, exclusive neighborhoods or veterans' organizations, they are all structures that allow us to feel comfortable with others who are like us. They reinforce our perceptions, values, and ideas since the members think as we do, enjoy the same pursuits, and may even dress in a similar style.

Minorities of all kinds—foreigners, homosexuals, blacks, or teenagers—also develop enclaves for their own safety from outsiders, some of whom may be actually threatening. They also may develop their own slang, traditions, and values to add to their sense of belonging. Such exclusive groups can serve as genuine sources of support, even as a bridge to the broader world.

With the help of counseling, support groups, and other personal development paths, we can clarify when our distancing is healthy and when it is isolating. We can examine our own personal responses of distancing and being close for examples of the way fear governs our relationships. As I observe my own fear in relationships, I am aware of creating fearful distance by avoiding contact, by withdrawing in anger or hurt, and by intellectualizing; and of creating fearful closeness by avoiding conflict, and by being overly accommodating, maybe too quickly agreeing with the opinion of others.

Primary Urges: Communion and Autonomy

The tendencies of closeness and distance, bonding and separation did not, however, begin as responses to fear.[8] They are primary urges that are as much a part of the natural rhythm of human interaction as breathing is to the human body. The first, the urge for communion, expresses our desire for togetherness, community, and "we-ness"; the second, the urge to autonomy, expresses our desire for distance, independence, and "I-ness." We are tempted to make a virtue or vice of one or the other. Yet each is essential to the existence of the other. Psychologist Harriet Goldhor Lerner puts it this way: "Only through our connectedness to others can we really know and enhance the self. And only through working on the self can we begin to enhance our connectedness to others."[9]

When we move from theory to the living documents of human lives, we realize that a perfect balance between "I-ness" and "we-ness" is not achievable. As complex as it may be, the quest for intimacy leads to a constant navigating between our need to be separate and our yearning to be close. This is the dance of intimacy.

Story of Julie and Michael
Julie and Michael are a couple in their forties. They have just sent the younger of their two children to college on a scholarship. During the early years of their marriage, Julie spent much of her time playing the traditional woman's role, devoting her energies to their growing children and their house, and supporting Michael in his position as a general manager for a large retail business, a job that he detested. Five years ago, Julie began to work as a substitute teacher in a local high school. After three years she was offered a full-time teaching position in the same school, a position she readily accepted.

Two years ago, after much discussion between the pair and bolstered by the additional income from Julie's full-time employment, Michael began his own small business. Although he has not regretted the change, he has often had second thoughts because of the demanding twelve-hour days he puts in and the anxious nights.

Julie felt challenged and exhilarated in her teaching responsibilities and was making new friends through her job. Although she occasionally complained about Michael's preoccupation with work and his withdrawal at home, she generally filled her time with new friendships and interests. Michael, on the other hand, would share little of his business anxiety with Julie, feeling he needed to prove himself and not burden his family. Yet, inside, Michael felt alone and unsupported. He became hostile.

Julie's and Michael's situation appears to be the case of two people simply becoming preoccupied with their separate interests. But beneath the obvious, there is a playing out of the familiar drama of separateness and closeness.

Julie's life path, as she watches her children move away from home and into their own adult years, is heading for new directions. The positive steps she has taken in appropriate distancing from her husband and family, by exploring new parts of herself and identifying new needs and interests, have lent growth and excitement to her life's possibilities. The job offer from her school was complimentary and raised her self-esteem. She feels proud to support Michael in seeking his own long-time dream, but Julie is confused by Michael's hostile behavior.

On the other hand, Michael is discovering that during this time of family transitions, the familiar and comfortable structures that had surrounded him for so many years are being dismantled. He is questioning his capabilities and his worth in this new business enterprise at the same time that Julie's new responsibilities and interests do not permit her to support him as she did during the earlier years of their marriage. His anger is surfacing as he touches on his dependency needs that he has never allowed himself to acknowledge; the result is pain, fear, and loneliness, which are threatening to him.

It does not occur to Michael to ask Julie to return to her part-time schedule so he can have her back. For one thing, such an action would not be sensitive to twentieth-century mores; for another, it would rob the couple of the financial cushion that has permitted Michael's business risk. He covers these threatening feelings with feelings of anger. The anger emerges in indirect ways as he distances himself physically from his wife. In conversation he replies to her briefly or sarcastically. Julie, who does not want a divorce and actually feels content in her new explorations, initiated counseling.

Both Michael and Julie recognize with a therapist's help that their marriage has moved into a transitional stage and that they must develop new communication methods to resolve the demands of their new identities. Michael has begun to understand that he chose not to share his feelings and business difficulties in order to protect Julie. He has begun to identify what he needs from her. This is a new pattern for both of them. In the early years of their marriage, Julie had become quite adept in learning to anticipate Michael's needs and improvised a safe and secure atmosphere at home.

It is a big step for Michael to see that he has been hiding his need for support and closeness behind a guise of self-sufficiency. He also has learned that some of his expectations about his wife's behavior are unrealistic. Although Julie empathizes with Michael's struggles, she is not the best source of support in dealing with his business problems. He might better discuss them with a peer or mentor. He has become able to address his feelings directly with Julie by saying, "I miss you being here, and I need your support." As he is able to identify just how he needs support from her, the pair agreed to take fifteen minutes every other day just to talk about what was going on with each of them. Michael also has become a part of a local chamber of commerce, where he can discuss the problems of new business development.

Julie has learned that although her need for distance at this time is appropriate and correct, it would be helpful for her to remain aware of how her choices affect others who are close to her. She also is learning not to interpret the responses of others as necessarily opposed to her healthy distancing, but to look at them as opportunities to practice new communication skills and to grow in yet another direction. Once Michael realized that Julie saw the changes and feelings he was experiencing, he was able to be genuinely supportive of her goals.

The story of Michael and Julie illustrates the dynamics of distance and closeness needed in every relationship. In the beginning, Michael called for distance and autonomy in the marriage as he focused on his career and personal concerns; Julie wanted closeness and togetherness, focusing on their children and Michael. It was only after circumstances permitted Julie to affirm her need for a separate identity that Michael was faced with his repressed need for closeness. Such shifts in the equilibrium of a relationship often create tension and a sense of confusion. Yet these times of redefinition of the distance-closeness dynamic also provide an opportunity for each partner to expand awareness of hidden needs for autonomy and attachment.

It is important in such transitional times that previously hidden needs are discussed and negotiated. Without such discussion the two people involved rely on mind reading ("she should know I need time to myself") or defiance ("I have a right to more attention"). In the case of Julie and Michael, the transition in their marriage took place over time, and they had the wisdom to discuss their changing needs. For others, the changes come more traumatically.

Approach/Avoidance Maneuver

Most of the time, one partner in a relationship will center on one of the primary needs: one will advocate for closeness, pursuing togetherness; the other will espouse separateness, retreating into autonomy.[10] Frequently there are flips in this pattern, often to the astonishment of those involved and those observing. The pursuer will see a need for separate space and will begin to distance him- or herself; the distancer will discover a need for closeness and begin to pursue the other. Sometimes these reversals are brief, almost a relief from the typical position; other times the switches are more dramatic and permanent. This "dance" of approach-avoidance[11] is common as people try to deal with the need for distance or for closeness.

The experience of Andrea and Pete demonstrates this reversal pattern in a striking way. They had been married for two years when they first came for counseling. Andrea had quit her job shortly after the marriage to devote time to creating a comfortable home. In the beginning sessions, Andrea would complain about Pete's frequent absences from home, his preoccupation with sports, and his resistance to shared activities. Pete would respond with predictable comments, justifying his need for time to himself and would counter Andrea's complaints by saying that she did not take an interest in his activities. They were clearly at an impasse.

Although on the surface their issue was one of control, focused on how they would spend their time, the underlying unresolved issue was, How did one want the other to be involved in his or her life? Andrea resolved this by announcing in the third session that she was no longer interested in talking about Pete's uninvolvement. In fact, she reported feeling happily disinterested in pursuing common activities and said she was experiencing a great sense of relief in accepting things as they were. She also had decided to resume her long-dormant interest in drama and theater, and intended to take a course at the local community college. Pete's initial response was relief, and he expressed support for Andrea's personal pursuits. But Andrea also withdrew emotionally, saying she had lost feeling for Pete.

Pete began to complain about their lack of sexual intimacy and expressed alarm at Andrea's lack of feeling for him. Andrea responded with an uncharacteristic detachment toward Pete, advising him not to expect much from her. Although Andrea did not invite him, Pete began to accompany her to church on Sunday mornings, an activity he had previously adamantly resisted. He also continued, without much success, to engage her in conversation about their relationship. Meanwhile, Andrea expanded her interests and friendships outside the marriage. Within the marriage Andrea and

Pete retained about the same distance in their relationship, although their positions as distancer and pursuer had clearly changed.

There are complex reasons for the switch in Andrea and Pete's relationship, and each partner developed a set of complementary steps in their approach-avoidance dance. When they married, Pete had not been prepared for a joint relationship and continued many activities he had enjoyed during his single years. Neither partner directed energy into strengthening their relationship as a couple. As the months passed, Andrea had difficulty in dealing with her feelings of anger and frustration so she withdrew. As Pete experienced the results of her withdrawal, he felt abandoned and began clinging to her.

A Developmental View

To understand how these primary needs for separateness and closeness arise as fears in our relationships, we need to understand what seeded our responses in the original relationships with our families. Developmental psychologists have helped us understand some of the stages of childhood development that affect our present relationships.[12] We will focus on two of those stages that especially bear on the issue of separation and closeness.

The symbiotic stage, between two months and seven months of age, is a phase of attachment and intense unity. It describes a stage in an infant's life where the "I" is not yet separate from the "not-I," the inside not distinct from the outside.[13] In this stage an infant experiences a yearning for connection with its caretakers.[14] This yearning becomes the metaphor for the experience of being closely bonded to another human being, and it follows us into our adult relationships. As the bonding stage progresses, the infant grows aware of the separate existence of other people. Yet, even in periods of separation, the infant maintains a sense of attachment, a feeling of being both distinct and connected; this is crucial to future relationships.[15]

As the infant grows so does its sense of separateness and the ability to do things independently, which is the stage of autonomy and independence. It is a time for exploration and reaching out.

The child delights in escaping from being held, in playing at a distance from its mother.[16] The child experiences a growing sense of autonomy and independent achievement. Bader and Pearson stress the importance at this stage of the caretaker's respecting the child's need for separation and expressing exhilaration at the child's accomplishments.[17] A child successfully emerging from this period has acquired the rudiments for acting and living independently and a strong sense of self.

Very early in life, infants intuitively understand that they have endings, or boundaries. They explore their hands and feet by trying to fit a chubby foot into their mouths, perhaps, or by stretching for an intriguing toy hanging from their crib just out of reach. In this way they begin to understand where they end and others begin, a concept central to their developing a sense of "I-ness."

It is to be hoped that each of us can grow through these stages of childhood development into a sense of security in the reliability of the world along with trust in our capacity to act effectively and independently. Trust in ourselves and the world becomes the foundation for our ability for emotional attachment and for affirming ourselves as individuals.

However, it is a tragic irony of life (expressed in the biblical image of the human fall from grace) that we emerge also as wounded persons. Even if we are not the walking wounded, who experienced childhood trauma and suffering, who were raised by alcoholic or abusive parents; even if we were raised in secure and nurturing homes, we still carry the "invisible scars of childhood."[18] This is true, according to therapist Harville Hendrix, "because from the time you were born you were a complex, dependent creature with a never-ending cycle of needs. . . . And no parents, no matter how devoted, are able to respond perfectly to all of these changing needs."[19] It is also true that caretakers bear their own wounds, passed on in subtle and not-so-subtle ways to their children. (We will deal with some of the limiting and wounding messages conveyed from parents to children in the next chapter.) It is the unfinished business of the past, including the wounds we carry, that reemerges in our present relationships as fearful distance and fearful closeness.

Fearful Distance

For some people, it is the fear of the loss of self, of engulfment, that disrupts their relationships. These people have often been reared in families where there was little permission to be an individual, to have one's own thoughts and feelings, to explore one's own space. As children and as adults, people may be aware of the reasons they feel invaded, manipulated, or controlled in relationships. Such persons live with a fear of being trapped, of being forever entangled in a relationship where "we" engulfs the "I."

The fear of engulfment leads some people to seek fearful distance in relationships, to avoid emotional and physical closeness. Fearful distance can be expressed through chronic daydreaming or fantasizing, or through the person's disappearing into the garage, the television, housework, a career, or the computer. Isolators, or distancers, can become expert at avoidance tactics and can point to quite reasonable excuses for being absent or unavailable: a busy work schedule, perhaps, or a large house that demands constant cleaning. Most of the reasons for avoidance are familiar and innocuous, such as a love of sports or an intrigue with soap operas. Even a serious volunteer, a person on every committee in the community, can be a distancer, as well as the one who falls asleep in the chair every night. Some other ways of avoidance are physically dangerous. People who drink and use drugs risk alcoholism and addiction. Withdrawal can also be emotionally dangerous for those who withdraw sexually or refuse to touch or be touched. These tactics of avoidance do not only keep us at a distance from others but also from our own emotional life.

We can achieve distance by provoking an argument or finding fault in the other person, which justifies moving back from and sometimes out of relationships. Some people simply avoid closeness by keeping so occupied that there is no time or energy for talking, holding, or making love.

When I met Fred and Nancy, they had honed into a fine art their pattern of maintaining distance from each other. I discovered that from the beginning of their twenty-five-year marriage, they had kept separate bank accounts, had pursued separate interests, including community involvement, and had made love only rarely—and not at all during the last three years. Nancy was quite involved with church activities and service projects, especially during the holidays; Fred spent a great deal of time at the neighborhood bar with his old cronies, reliving good times of their youth.

They were friendly with two other couples, and the six of them would take vacation cruises twice yearly. At home, Fred and Nancy were a fixture, together for golfing, parties, and other leisure activities. With such an arrangement, they ingeniously avoided being alone together. During the times when they were alone at home, Nancy invariably stayed in one room, reading the mystery stories she liked, and Fred retired to his carpentry workshop. The only times they were seen together without their adult friends were for the activities of their two children. Their neighbors viewed them as totally devoted to their children. They faithfully attended the children's sports events, music recitals, and other activities that spotlighted their children. It is not surprising, then, that when their second child was preparing to leave home they sought counseling. Nancy had complained of depression. During the sessions, their relationship became clear. But even after several weeks of therapy, they remained unable to acknowledge their fear of closeness. In the therapy sessions, when the subject of sharing activities was broached, they would both quickly say how much they enjoyed being with other people. They would not discuss the possibility of spending time just with each other. Later, Fred and Nancy created the space they needed by inviting an exchange student to live with them.

For some people who fear closeness, the linchpin in their relationship is tested when unexpected and additional responsibilities emerge as part of a crisis or life change. For example, changes that accompany the arrival of a child into the family can be perceived as overwhelming.

The marriage—and the separation—of Ruth and Jim show how fears of responsibility in an emotional commitment can contribute to a distorted need for separateness.

Shortly before their senior year, Ruth met Jim, a high school sports' star who was well liked by his classmates. They married a year after graduation. During the first year of marriage, both experienced some sense of normal disillusionment as they settled into day-to-day living. Jim pursued his job as a computer technician, and Ruth kept busy with a part-time clerical job while she used her free time to paint, paper, and renovate their old house.

In the second year, Ruth became pregnant unexpectedly. She was surprised, but happy; Jim, however, was not in favor of the pregnancy. He began to spend more time away from home, drinking with friends at the local bar. It was not unusual for Jim to keep his wife waiting at the dinner table, where the home-cooked meal turned cold. Ruth suspected that Jim was having an affair, and as her pregnancy moved into the fifth month, her fears were confirmed.

Jim then moved in with the woman who had claimed his attentions, but that affair ended and he moved into his own apartment. Ruth gave birth to a little girl, but allowed Jim to visit with the child.

It had not been Ruth's pattern to make demands on Jim but rather to be solicitous of his welfare, especially in their early dating days. Jim had felt threatened by the responsibility of emotional involvement and was effectively able to avoid real emotional commitment with both women in his life, as well as with his child.

Fearful Closeness

On the other hand, there are those whose greatest fear is the loss of love, that is, abandonment or rejection. They are the wounded who grew up with caretakers not equipped to give them emotional support, people who would often withdraw in the face of a child's needs. Children so deprived often grow into adults who have a craving for closeness but cannot form a close relationship. In them the "I" is sacrificed in the interest of maintaining the "we."

The fear of abandonment leads such people to fearful closeness, a closeness borne out of a fear of not being loved. Fearful closeness can be expressed in several ways, for example, in an addictive clinging, in a persistent helplessness, or in a compulsive helpfulness. People of this kind tend to merge with others, to become fusers or pursuers in relationships. They advocate togetherness and minimize differences.

Although such advocates' endeavors to merge with another are a response to the fear of being alone, more often than not their efforts result only in more isolation. Consider, for example, George, who was constantly frustrated in his efforts to establish a lasting and caring relationship with a woman. (In many ways, George is a counterpart to Laura, whom we introduced in the first chapter.) He is a congenial and attractive man who is generally well liked by his friends and colleagues. Most women would describe George as "a catch" at first meeting. George, for his part, would pursue women with phone calls and invitations. Yet in his relationships with them, those he labeled his most likely prospects would invariably leave after a few weeks or months.

When this happened, he would express dissatisfaction with the particular woman and terminate the relationship. Further investigation, however, revealed that George was demanding of women, insisting that they be available to him without regard for their own needs or wishes. He expected, for instance, that they reserve their Friday and Saturday nights as date nights with him. When one girlfriend, Sharon, told him she could not spend a Friday night with him because she was planning to celebrate a college friend's birthday, George complained and accused her of not caring for him as much as she had claimed. When another friend Mindy told him that she felt hungry for Chinese food, rather than for the fare at the Italian restaurant they usually frequented, George took her casual comment as a personal affront and scarcely spoke to her for the remainder of the evening.

Cynthia told George that she could not see him for two weeks because she had decided to take time away from work to visit her elderly parents in another state. George voiced resentment about her trip and grumbled when she asked him to drive her to the airport.

George constantly interpreted any difference of opinion or of desire from the women in his life as rejection and a lack of support. He responded by withdrawing physically or by pouting about the woman's lack of concern. At some point he would have a talk with each woman, telling her the relationship wasn't working.

A look into George's background reveals some significant items. George had had an indulgent mother who died tragically in a car accident when he was a child of ten. His father was distant and only noticed George when he "proved his worth" in school with high grades and awards. George's emotional deprivation filtered every interaction with women, yet he was not enough in touch with his emotional needs to express them directly nor to gain perspective about the needs of others.

In other couples, fearful closeness can result in a merging of their identities. For these couples, there is very little "I," only "we"; they take literally the phrase "the two shall become one." It is common for such couples to speak of "us" even when they mean "me," to speak for each other in conversations, and to anticipate what the other thinks and wants. Conflict and disagreements are often avoided because differences of opinion or emotion are seen as threatening to the relationship.[20]

Lucinda and Dick are a couple in their late fifties whose entire lives have centered on their three children, now grown and with families of their own. The divorce of their youngest daughter has been painful for them, especially since they genuinely liked the young man she had married and had supported him financially as he advanced in his educational goals. Because of their concerns about their daughter's divorce, they have also contributed money for child care for their two grandchildren, and Lucinda has made a habit of rising at dawn each day to ferry the grandchildren from their house to a child care facility, a thirty-mile round trip that she repeats in the evening.

Other than Lucinda's attention to this chore, the couple spend all their time together, whether the task is grocery shopping, yard work, or visiting with friends. In counseling, they express hurt that their two older children have moved out of state and that the daughter whom they have helped financially and emotionally doesn't spend a great deal of time with them. As they share their common distress, it seems at first that they agree about everything. Both lack any sense of why these circumstances have happened to them and feel connected with each other by their distress.

It is only after several months that Lucinda begins to acknowledge that the couple do not have identical feelings about their children, their children's problems, and what to do about them. As differences begin to emerge slowly, Dick expresses a wish to move to a retirement community in a warmer climate, a move that would make the couple unavailable to help their daughter for child care arrangements. Lucinda can't imagine leaving her daughter to "fend for herself." The focus on their children and grandchildren appears to be the unifying element that has kept Dick and Lucinda together.

It is important to distinguish between the fearful distance being described here and that of the early stage of romantic love. In the beginning of a romantic relationship, it is common and desirable that the couple take time for bonding, for accentuating their similarities and minimizing their differences. But inevitably the differences begin to emerge, and in a healthy relationship the partners can recognize them and accommodate them. In fearful distancing people deny their disillusionment when facing the differences, and create a false and fearful closeness that stifles their autonomy.

Space in Togetherness

Kahlil Gibran's words, "Let there be space in your togetherness,"[21] are frequently quoted in wedding services. They carry a fundamental truth: If there is no space, there can be no togetherness, but without togetherness there is no relationship. Throughout this chapter we have been focusing on the distancing and closeness that result from fear, especially the fears of engulfment and abandonment; yet distancing and closeness, separateness and togetherness, "I-ness" and "We-ness," represent the basic movements of a relationship, the primary elements of intimacy.

How do we achieve appropriate distance and closeness in our relationships? We need first to acknowledge that there is no simple measure of what is the right amount of space in togetherness. We all differ in our needs for closeness and distance. Through self-awareness and insight from others, however, we can discern our own pattern of fearful reaction, our own needs for autonomy and attachment. We can also recognize and empathize with these needs in others.

Cultivating our "I-ness," our distinctive sense of identity, involves learning to recognize and express our feelings, our thoughts, our dreams, needs, and desires. We can be who we are without depending on the validation of others. It is learning to say no and yes, not out of compliance or defiance, but out of a genuine sense of our own preferences and values. It is accepting, respecting, and appreciating our separateness and differences. It is also experimenting with new behaviors, forgiving ourselves, affirming our giftedness, acknowledging our unique contribution and destiny.

Enhancing our "We-ness" means developing our ability to respect and respond effectively to the needs, opinions, thoughts, and views of others. It is knowing what and when something is appropriately said or done. It is learning tolerance and cooperation. It is approaching others without judgement or bias. In this way we create a safe place for people to express their feelings and desires.

Some personal boundaries are constant and others change according to mood, circumstance, and time. We are well acquainted with invasion of physical boundaries, for instance, when children are touched sexually or threatened or violated with physical harm. In dealing with a child's misbehavior, aware and caring parents take corrective measures that do not involve hitting, striking, or slapping. But personal boundaries are violated in more subtle ways that prevent children from claiming what is inherently their own—their bodies and their selves.

Aunt Sarah, for example, directs her young nephew Jason to kiss her friends to show them how friendly he is. "Give this lady a hug," she says, "and give Uncle Tim a kiss." She then thrusts this three-year-old into the face of strangers—people who are her friends, not his. Jason has not developed a relationship with these people, nor is he able to interact with them on an adult level. Also, he is not given the opportunity to decline. After willingly hugging several people at the party Jason begins pulling away, whining a bit as he puts his small hand out, warding away these big faces. Aunt Sarah apologizes for his reluctance, explaining, "He's cranky and tired—it's time for a nap, isn't it?"

If this kind of treatment persists as Jason grows older, he may lose the idea that he is entitled to ownership of his own body. He may feel obliged to let others touch him as they please and may risk molestation by a person who should not be trusted. On the other hand, Jason may pull inward, seeing any expression of affection as an invasion of his privacy and have difficulty offering or receiving affection.

We also can violate others' emotional boundaries by insisting on a particular temperament in the house, workplace, or community. Here is a typical home situation that's common in many families. Dad has had a busy and demanding day at the office and arrives home feeling tired and maybe even a bit grumpy. But his twin girls, Sis and Lorna, are bounding around the house, giggling and joking. They were just notified that they've been accepted for a scholarship to a summer music camp. They want to talk about how much fun this camp experience should be.

If Dad frowns at their joy and gives them the message that they must suppress their gladness during the times when he is tired, they will feel guilty. Families and groups who respect each other's boundaries are able to respect differences of opinion, preferences, emotional states, and other individual experiences.

Theologian Paul Tillich speaks of "the courage to be" in his book by the same name, and heralds "the courage to be as oneself," the courage to affirm ourselves as distinguishable, incomparable, free, self-determining persons. We might call this the courage to be "I." Yet "the courage to be" also includes "the courage to be a part," the courage to be a part of our structured universe, the world in which we live, including a part of intimate relationships. We can call this second element the courage to be "We." Both forms of courage comprise "the courage to be"; both are expressions of intimacy.[22]

If we wish to invite intimacy in our lives, we must move beyond fear. But we do not have to wait for fear to disappear before we can take steps to affirm ourselves or to reach out to others. Rather, we can courageously acknowledge the fear we feel and take risks in making contact with others. Facing fears of engulfment or abandonment, yet moving ahead in trust, is an expression of the courage to be. Chronic fear that is unacknowledged and unexpressed forces us into the polarities of fearful distance and fearful closeness.

Intimacy, however, is more than balancing distance and closeness. Henri Nouwen, whose words head this chapter, reminds us: "Intimacy . . . is a way of being in which the tension between distance and closeness is dissolved."[23] Intimacy is a way of being in relationship without losing a sense of our distinctive self. In intimacy, we are not merged to another so as to lose our separate identity; there is an indwelling of our lives in one another so that even with a separation of space and time we remain a part of each other.[24] When Jesus says, "Abide in me as I abide in you,"[25] he is inviting us into a way of being, an experience of indwelling in which there is not tension between the I and the we. We have moved beyond fear into intimacy.

Finally, intimacy is not an achievement, although it requires our awareness and effort. "Intimacy is less a thing than an event or happening,"[26] says theologian William Johnston. Love, trust, and commitment create the safe space necessary for intimacy. It is only when we find ourselves in the safe space, where we experience love without judgment, trust without conditions, and commitment without end, that we can let go of our fears of abandonment and engulfment.

We can experience such moments of safety and grace in our relationships with one another, during times when we are spontaneously and playfully close and respectfully distant. Yet the love that ultimately drives out our fear has its source beyond our human loves. When the psalmist writes: "Even though I walk through the darkest valley, I fear no evil; for you are with me," we are reminded that even in our times of deepest isolation we can trust that we are not alone and will never be abandoned.

But within this sacred relationship, it is still the "I" who walks through the valley; it is still my individual journey to make. It is in our relationship with the sacred Other that we are given the model of intimacy. And it is Jesus, in whom the fullness of the Other dwells, who invites us to abide in Him as He abides in us. Jesus is a safe place, a place of intimacy, which is beyond fear.

Chapter Three

Escapes from Intimacy

Intimacy is two people being exposed at the same time, showing the good and bad parts they usually keep hidden.
Eileen McCann

Intimacy is putting aside the masks we wear the rest of our lives.
Lillian B. Rubin

Family Messages

Long before the first screen kiss stirs our adolescent hormones, we have already been imprinted thousands of times by messages our families give us about adult behavior. These familial messages define how we must think, feel, and talk with others, and they bear on our ability to experience the joy and pain of loving relationships, particularly affecting our responses to those we most deeply love.

The essential job of a parent is to help children define their experience of being alive and learn effective and appropriate ways of communicating that experience with others. Every family has rules about the expression of life's experiences. Most probably we are trained first in the expression of feelings, as other means of expression—thoughts and observations—demand later skills of verbalizing. These messages about feelings are communicated in a variety of ways. In abusive families, rules about feelings are unusually rigid and obvious: children are punished physically or cruelly ridiculed for crying or expressing anger. In most families, however, the response to unacceptable feelings is less severe and sometimes even quite subtle.

Lucie, for instance, grew up in a family where anger was seldom acknowledged or expressed. She recalls how she became angry when her younger sister, Lynda, barged into her bedroom in her absence and took an article of clothing and a music tape without asking. She had yelled at her sister and asked their mother to make her sister stay out of her room. But Lucie's mother told her that "life is too short to argue" and recommended that Lucie be less possessive about her belongings and more willing to share them with her sister. The father kept out of the fray, but told Lucie to listen to her mother. In that family, anger was not seen as a justified reaction to invasion of privacy, and neither parent offered guidance in healthy ways to voice anger and solve conflict.

The most potent messages, however, are not given verbally but in subtle, nonverbal ways. Often the verbal messages are contradicted by the nonverbal, and the nonverbal carry the day. The givers of these messages, for the most part, are not aware they are teaching children about feelings, attitudes, and behaviors.

As the baby of the family, Millie often felt lonely growing up in a house where her three teenage brothers were busy with high school activities, sports, and their friends. Her solicitous mother seemed interested in Millie's welfare and often told Millie that she could come to her to talk about anything. But when Millie began to talk about being sad or lonely, her mother would take her on a shopping trip to buy her a new doll or a pretty dress. Millie discerned that loneliness was an unwanted feeling, to be erased as quickly as possible, and that material possessions provided a way of dealing with painful feelings. Millie's mother, no doubt, was uncomfortable with her own loneliness; she could not explain to her daughter that sometimes people are lonely because painful feelings are, in fact, a part of living.

Messages are also effectively conveyed with assignation, a word or phrase that assigns a quality to a person. When Mary was growing up, she often heard herself described as a shy person. The label became her attribute. Mary soon began to define herself as shy and began to think and act accordingly.[1] When Randy, as a toddler, burst out with an angry tantrum, his behavior was quickly excused with, "He's so tired." Through the years, Randy learned to mislabel his feeling. He started to confuse exhaustion with the anger that he didn't recognize in himself.[2]

Another method of family communication is through directives. For instance, a family may tell children, "You shouldn't feel that way" or There are some things that shouldn't be said." Such messages also may apply to gender: "Girls don't act that way!" or "Boys don't cry!"[3] Children might be admonished to "Put on a happy face!" or "Where's that smile?" So the obedient child learns to cover up unacceptable feelings with a cheerful mask. If the family is more familiar with sadness and guilt but not with anger, children might be told, "You're not really angry." Some families even use religion to underline their injunctions as children are told to "turn the other cheek" (in the face of conflict or disagreement); "Don't be proud!" (directed at any comment perceived as bragging); or "Sex is beautiful, but don't talk about it" (conveying that sex is an unclean subject).

Family messages are also certainly given by example. Children are keen observers of their parents' living messages. They observe their choices, the rules they live by, their actions, and their attitudes. Joe, for example, had only once seen his father become teary, the day he received a letter of the sudden death from a heart attack of an Army buddy. His father's tears and embarrassment quickly turned to anger; he yelled at his curious son to go to his room. When Joe was in seventh grade and his favorite grandmother died, he remembers going behind a small shed in his backyard to cry. He then recalls sneaking into his house and carefully making his way to the bathroom to wash his face and clear up any evidence of tears. Without ever having been told directly, Joe had already concluded that it was not manly to show tears.

In another family, the members were free in expressing anger and irritation, but found it difficult to show tenderness. The children learned that a jab in the arm or a wrestling match on the living room rug was the kind of attention or recognition they could expect from adults.

We also inherit rules about how to state our wants and needs. If it is not permissible to express needs openly and directly—perhaps we might be labeled selfish or greedy—we reroute feelings into unconscious means of getting our needs met. Often anger or sulking is a way of asserting our need for attention. Those who regularly show a sad face, perhaps playing the martyr, have learned to use unhappiness to manipulate others to attend to them. The story of Julie is typical. In counseling sessions she would often complain about how she felt taken advantage of by her family and friends. When I asked her what she wanted from her family or friends that she was not receiving, Julie would hesitate and act confused. It became apparent that when confronted with questions related to her wants, Julie would be vague and stumble for an answer. A brief excursion into her past helped clarify the reasons for her hesitation and vagueness. In Julie's family, people did not ask directly for what they wanted. Although the rule "Don't want!" was not openly stated, it was known by each member of the family. Direct statements of wants or needs were seen as aggressive and selfish. Julie learned to whine as a way of stating her needs and to sulk when she did not get what she wanted. Now, as an adult, she still follows the family rule, but the reason for it has long since been hidden from her consciousness.

It has been said that whoever discovered water was most definitely not a fish. Family rules regarding feelings, thinking, and behaving become our assumed reality, an intricate part of our internal environment that we are seldom aware of. Yet it is within that environment of hidden rules that we make the key decisions about ourselves and our relationships with others. As we learn these survival rules as children and adjust to the emotional environment of the family, we become clever and creative in finding ways to avoid forbidden emotions, thoughts, or behaviors. We arrive at certain conclusions, or beliefs, that define who we are in relationship to ourselves and others. Yet these very decisions that were fitting when we were growing up, which may have helped us as children survive physically and emotionally, can become inappropriate, even damaging, to relationships at a later time. These decisions have a common element: They come out of the unfinished business of our past, from a period when we were unaware of many of the reasons for our actions and feelings. Sometimes, indeed, our responses derive from misunderstanding or misinformation. A very hurtful, not uncommon example, is that of a child magically assuming his own anger caused the death of a loved parent. Our responses to inadequate parenting can result in our becoming incomplete people, growing up to minimize our anger, fear, sadness, or joy. We develop conditioned patterns "that cloud our awareness, distort our feelings, and restrict our capacity to be open to life and to love."[4]

The Masks of Intimacy

The responses we learn in our families become a kind of prism, through which we see and through which we assign meaning to the events and relationships in our lives. These responses are incorporated into stories we tell ourselves and live out day by day.[5] They may be assimilated into the script of our stories in the form of directives:

- "Don't get close to people or you'll get hurt."
- "Don't ask for what you need because you'll only be disappointed."
- "If you say what you feel, people won't like you."

Our stories are often lived out as patterns of behavior that emphasize the extremes of either giving or receiving. We can learn, for example, to live out stories that permit us only to take care of others and to ignore our own needs; or stories that present us as helpless, dependent on the resources of others to survive.

Although these patterns are frequently identified with being intimate, they lack the mutuality and vulnerability that distinguish true intimacy. Behind the masks of caretaking and dependency are concealed the legitimate needs for giving and receiving.

Caretaking: Focus on Others

Joan's eyes fill with tears as she speaks about a confrontation with her thirty-year-old daughter, Ann, the oldest of her three children. Embarrassed by her tears, she quickly explains that she is angry, not sad. Since her husband's death, Joan has devoted her life to her children. She has dated only occasionally and never considers remarrying. In the mother-daughter confrontation, Ann had accused Joan of interfering with her relationship with Allen, a man Ann had known for a year. Joan admits she did not approve of Allen but says she was offended at being labeled "interfering." Joan insists her comments to Ann were expressions of concern that her daughter not be hurt.

This episode contains familiar elements of the entanglement of caretaking and intimacy. Author Lillian Rubin says directly that "nurturance is not intimacy. It may be connected to intimacy, may even sometimes be a result of it, but the two are distinct and separate phenomena."⁶ There is a difference between nurturance as an expression of intimacy, which we will call "caregiving," and nurturance as a mask of intimacy, which we will refer to as "caretaking." Caretaking begins when we take control through caring, binding another person to us through obligation or guilt. We exploit or are exploited by the dependency of others, often with the unspoken intention of not being left alone.

Joan is, indeed, a caring mother, and she has made many sacrifices on behalf of her children. Yet she has also frequently become interfering with Ann, offering unsolicited advice, expressing unwelcome opinions, and otherwise trying to influence her daughter's decisions. At times, Ann had mildly protested her mother's interferences. Until the confrontation over her relationship to Allen, Ann had been reluctant to be openly critical. She hadn't wanted to offend her mother. Although Ann had occasionally complained to close friends about her mother's expectations and comments, she had never before so forcefully expressed her anger. At first Joan was dazed by her daughter's words and genuinely confused at being labeled interfering. It was as though her whole identity as a mother was called into question. With some counseling, however, and the help of a close friend, Joan recognized her overinvestment in her daughter's life and acknowledged her anxiety about Ann's growing independence. Joan in time perceived her own behavior as a reaction to her anxiety and as interference with her daughter's right to make her own decisions.

The motives for caretaking can be as diverse as "a way of gaining love, of palliating fears of abandonment, of ensuring safety and security."[7] Whatever the motives, the underlying incentive is anxiety and insecurity. It is characteristic of caretakers that they tend to—

- Overidentify with other people's feelings, needs, and problems and ignore their own;
- Feel uncomfortable when another is struggling with a problem they assume they can solve;
- Feel constrained to offer advice, to rescue, and to take away the pain or discomfort of the other person;
- Seldom ask the other person what he or she needs or wants but instead make assumptions about what the other person needs.

The confrontation between the mother and daughter proved to be a turning point for them. It often takes a crisis to disrupt a familiar pattern and to provide opportunity for fresh insight into an unconscious process. Joan and Ann's confrontation was such a crisis and opportunity. But insight and change required self-reflection and determination. In facing this crisis, Joan decided to move beyond being offended, to understanding Ann's need to be her own person. By listening to Ann, clarifying her intentions, and avoiding giving advice, Joan began to affirm her daughter's ability to make decisions. Joan also learned that she avoided her own unmet needs for companionship and nurture by focusing on Ann and her other children and that she seldom would ask for or accept the support of others. Having been raised in a family where stating wants and discussing feelings were discouraged, Joan, as the oldest daughter, had gained recognition by caring for her two younger brothers and sister. Caretaking had become for her a way of life.

Bolstered with new confidence by her act of protest, Ann willingly discussed her feelings and wants more openly with her mother. She learned to use her anger as a signal, as her angel, as she put it, to help her identify her unstated wants. As time passed, Ann came to appreciate the experience and insight of her mother, and to ask clearly for her mother's observations and suggestions.

Because caretakers focus on the needs of others as they navigate through life, they often find themselves depleted of energy and frequently disappointed and dejected when their efforts to help others go unheeded. It is typical for caretakers to feel hurt and unappreciated and for these feelings to be amplified into depression or anger.

At the age of forty, Henry is coming to realize that he has been assigned the family role of caretaker for his aging parents. When his seventy-four-year-old father suffered a serious heart attack, it was simply understood that Henry would be the one to ferry his mother from her rural home to the metropolitan hospital for daily visits.

His brother, a successful TV anchorman who lived in a city hundreds of miles away, explained that he couldn't take time from his demanding job. His sister, who also lived in another state, said that responsibilities for her husband, teenage son, and club took her time and energy. She promised to do what she could from a distance, but she and her mother didn't get along. Henry, who is a self-employed writer with his business in his home, put aside his own work during this family emergency to make the daily trips. Then he would struggle to find time to be with his wife, to take his toddler to the local day-care center, and to give attention to his older daughter from his first marriage.

As the pressures continued to build, Henry felt angry. He recalled the many weekends he had visited his siblings, helped them to paint their houses, build an outdoor deck, install a new bathroom. He realized that these family obligations had taken time away from his own job, drained his immediate family's precarious savings, and prevented him from producing enough income to pay the bills that were piling up. Henry felt angry that his brother was not sympathetic to his financial needs and that his sister could not put aside personal differences with their mother to help out during this family emergency. He finally exploded, venting his feelings to his brother and sister.

Henry's father has since recovered from his heart attack, but his esiblings are not speaking to Henry. His parents, distressed that his angry words caused a rift in their family, also are not speaking to him. Henry, who is still angry, rebuffed an effort to make contact; he returned the Christmas presents his relatives sent him.

But Henry has taken the first important step in wholeness. He recognizes that his pattern of helpfulness has been at the expense of caring for himself and his family. Real growth, however, can take place only when Henry begins to explore the identity "he who helps" has given him. He may discover that through helpfulness he tries to connect with people; it is his way of showing that he cares about them. He also may discover that compulsive helpfulness can distract him from his own painful feelings and anxieties. Finally, he may begin to understand that he tends to draw people to him who are not generous givers and are needy.

In order for caretakers to move away from the victim role, they must identify their investment in the adulation and recognition of their rescuing behavior. Often caretakers need to feel angry in order to begin setting boundaries on their own behavior. They can do so without blaming others or separating emotionally from them. In Henry's case, he could say to his brother and sister, "I will no longer be the only one to tend to our parents' needs. I have to make a living, to support my family. I also want you to know that I'm willing to come up with some alternative ways of supporting our parents. But I won't take care of them alone any longer."

A paradigm of the caretaker in the New Testament is Martha, the sister of Mary and Lazarus, and friend of Jesus. When on one occasion Jesus is visiting them and in deep conversation with Mary, Martha becomes angry, complaining that she is busy preparing the meal while her sister is free to talk with their guest. Caretakers frequently feel victimized by the freedom and lack of obligation of others. Martha may be as angry with Jesus for encouraging Mary's malingering as with Mary for taking time out from chores. According to the scripture, Martha is "distracted by her many tasks."[8] Jesus comments to her that she is "worried and distracted by many things" when only one thing is important: to sit, listen and, learn—in a word, to receive.

Caretakers tend to have difficulty in receiving; they connect with others primarily by being helpful and nurturing. They are the first to volunteer to serve on a committee, to visit the sick, and to fix a meal. They have trouble saying no to any request for help; giving is an obligation, a mandate. Nurturing and helping is the only way they justify themselves. Because caretakers are very uncomfortable receiving, they develop a kind of nonstick coating that diverts incoming support and care from others. They are uneasy being served or even being given a compliment.

Caretaking has been highly emphasized in the church. We are told, "It is more blessed to give than receive" or "Give till it hurts." Such an accent on caretaking has caused many people to feel guilty for feeling tired of giving. Some of us wonder if we are selfish for setting reasonable limits when trying to help someone who does not take responsibility for self-care. It is important to recall the times when Jesus resisted the pressure to attend to the sick and withdrew into solitude to replenish his own energy. Remember, too, that Jesus called upon the companionship of his disciples and friends during times of turmoil and transition, for example, in Gethsemane.[9]

On the other hand, caregiving (in contrast to caretaking) is mutual. The giving required in an intimate connection does not come as a response to internal or external demand. It moves freely between partners. Caregivers are able to receive without embarrassment or discomfort, and they are able to give generously without obligation. In relating to others, caregivers—

- Distinguish what other people feel, need, and think from what the caregivers feel, need, and think.
- Trust the ability of others to solve their own problems and affirm the right of others to make their own decisions.
- Resist giving advice or directives, but offer help by clarifying issues and affirming the resources of others.
- Provide support and encouragement to another without assuming responsibility for what the other decides.

There are, of course, situations when we are required to become more directive with people—for example, when a person needs protection or is developmentally or circumstantially dependent on others. Young children are the most obvious example of such people. But we can all find ourselves in dependent situations from time to time.

Dependence: Denial of Self-Empowerment

Besides the legitimately dependent person there are those who adopt a lifestyle of dependence. They lean on someone else to make decisions, to give them direction, and to assume responsibility for them. These folks connect to and become intimate with others primarily out of helplessness. But their connection is only a mask of intimacy, which we now turn to explore.

Masked dependents are those who do not trust their own facility and resources for life. They tend to discount their capacity to make sound judgements, to think clearly, to accomplish tasks. They often question their impressions, thoughts, and feelings about a given situation. They will then turn to others for validation.

It was only after her husband of thirty-five years had died that Donna learned to drive a car. "My husband Harold would take me wherever I needed to go," she explained to the counselor as she detailed the many ways she had depended on him. After her husband's sudden death of a heart attack two years before, Donna asked a friend to teach her to drive and another to tutor her in balancing her checkbook. During most of her marriage, Donna looked to her husband to make the major financial decisions. She did not know the extent or location of their investments. It had been enough for her to know Harold would provide for their future.

Donna has grown in confidence during the last two years. Without consultation or discussion she now takes on many tasks which her husband would have done. Donna is also discovering some intense personal anger when she thinks of missed opportunities for personal growth and for travel during the years of her marriage. She came to counseling because of the guilt she feels about being angry with her husband, whom she believes encouraged her helplessness. She recalled a scene, for example, when her husband joked in front of friends about her inability to add figures in the checkbook. Although she recalls laughing with the others, now Donna experiences the humiliation and embarrassment she had repressed.

Yet Donna muses, "I loved my husband very much, and I miss him desperately." It is difficult for her to reconcile loving him and being angry with him at the same time. Sometimes, Donna focuses her anger on herself: "How could I not stand up for myself?" "Why did I not get angry then?"

There is no culprit in this relationship. No doubt Harold had invested in Donna's being dependent, especially regarding money. He had taken many opportunities to discount Donna's intellect with comments like, "Math is just not your thing" and "Just let me do the thinking." And he had discouraged her independence with statements like, "You don't need to drive. It gives us a chance to be together."

By inviting Donna's dependence, Harold fortified his identity as the breadwinner in the family and protected himself from facing his own fear of being abandoned. Yet Donna benefited from her belief that Harold was in control. She had reinforced his position as the thinking partner by frequently deferring to his judgment. She felt secure knowing he would handle matters in their lives. It did not occur to her that she was paying a price for this security; she had experienced no anger, no loss of autonomy.

Perhaps the anger that Donna now experiences is partly related to feeling abandoned by her husband. But at a deeper level, Donna's anger is a voice of protest, which she could express only now that she has achieved a degree of detachment and a sense of herself as a separate individual. It is unlikely Donna could have risked being angry until she was satisfied that she could psychologically survive outside the marriage relationship. Paradoxically, she could only relate to Harold in an intimate way when she realized that her wholeness was not dependent on him.

It is not important that one of the parties in this relationship is deceased. As a telling line from the film *I Never Sang for My Father* puts it, "Death ends a life; it does not end a relationship." Sometimes in therapy the deceased must be raised in order for the living to complete unfinished business. For Donna, this took the form of a dialogue with Harold. Using an empty chair as the focus, she used the potency of her anger to declare her independence as a capable, thinking, feeling woman.

An example of the dependent in the New Testament is the invalid who had been lying by the pool of Bethzatha for thirty-eight years, looking for someone to assist him into the water so he could be healed. Dependence had become for him a way of life. "I have no one to put me into the pool," he says. And he continues, "While I am making my way, someone else steps down ahead of me." He believes he is a victim of circumstance and of the lack of concern on the part of others. Jesus' response to him comes in two forms. First, Jesus asks the startling question, "Do you want to be made well?" Even in such a situation, Jesus does not presume to know the man's wishes. And second, Jesus calls the man into a responsible act, "Stand up, take your mat and walk." The story gives not only the profile of the dependent, but also the response of Jesus, the caregiver.[10]

In relating to others, dependents tend to—

- Deny their own ability to feel, think, or decide and to look to others for advice, validation, and approval.
- Downplay their own competence and power with the belief that this is the best way to keep others in relationship.
- Underestimate their capability to make a positive difference in the lives of other people.

The story of Harold and Donna illustrates, also, the complementary nature of relationships. Dr. Murray Bowen, a pioneer in family therapy, has described the reciprocal pattern of relationships, pointing out that one partner will often tend to diminish the self by underfunctioning while the other creates a pseudo-self by overfunctioning. In the marriage of Harold and Donna, Harold clearly overfunctioned in the marriage and thereby created a pseudo-self, the "man of the house," while Donna disowned her ability to think and to act independently.

Donna's tendency to dependency should not conceal the fact we all have dependency needs, nor detract from our appreciating the limits of self-sufficiency. It is not a sign of weakness to recognize that we are of necessity dependent on one another. It is a strength that draws us into community with others.

Need for Balance

Both of the negative tendencies we have been discussing—caretaking and dependency—are extreme expressions of the very normal and appropriate personal needs to give and to receive. Yet behind caretaking and dependency is a deeper imbalance that affects all levels of our existence. There are two main directions which this imbalance can take, each representing a specific form of denial. On the one hand is the denial of limitations. This occurs when people refuse to accept vulnerability, boundaries, and dependence on one another and on the Source of all life. Caretakers tend to deny their limitation by overemphasizing the nurturing and controlling dimensions of human interaction. In the long run, the denial of limitations is a desire to be superhuman. That leads to what theologian Reinhold Niebuhr calls the sin of pride, the temptation to play God.

On the other hand, dependents deny possibilities and retreat from discovering potentiality, from decision making, and from responsibility. They overemphasize their dependency and helplessness. In actuality, the denial of possibility is a desire to be subhuman. It leads to what Niebuhr called the sin of sensuality, the temptation to play worm.

Caretaking and dependency are part of the accommodation we made to our family of origin. Like the messages we absorbed as children, caretaking and dependency are ways we learned to adapt to the environment in which we were reared. Caretakers often were brought up to deny their own wants and feelings and to focus on the others'. The adults approved of caretakers for being little adults who learned to anticipate and accommodate to the needs of other family members. The children responded to messages that said,

"Don't be a child!" or "Don't want!" Grown-up caretakers find it hard to relate to others on a mutual basis. They link primarily to the neediness of others and seldom share their own vulnerability and pain. They may be great listeners and helpers, but reveal little of themselves.

Dependents, on the other hand, are often raised by those people who need to be needed. They incorporate the message "Don't grow up!" Often their strength and competence are belittled with comments such as, "You couldn't think your way out of a paper bag" or "You better marry a good man to take care of you." Dependents are not formed, however, only by way of occasional or casual remarks, but by a persistent demeaning of their capability, thinking, and perceptions.

Caretaking and dependency then are woven into the fabric of our lives; they become patterns of relating to the world and to one another that are not easily modified or changed. There are times when a person switches position. The caretaker will shift into dependence; the dependent, into a state of high functioning. Such shifts are usually a temporary relief from the predominate pattern. For example, Paul is a physician, well known for his diligent care of patients. He seldom takes vacations or a full day off from work. Last year Paul found himself the patient when appendicitis sent him to the emergency room of the hospital. During his brief hospital stay and the week of recuperation at home, Paul relished his dependency on his wife, Sarah, who stayed with him and waited on him.

Detaching from these patterns of caretaking and dependency may be very upsetting, an emotional death. Yet consistency in them masks our deepest feelings, thoughts, and behavior. It also prevents us from experiencing the new life of intimacy.

Taking Off the Masks

Behind the persona, or mask, we present to others is a hidden self made up of disowned and forbidden feelings, thoughts, and behaviors we have learned to camouflage. Often others see parts of us that remain hidden to ourselves; sometimes we suspect we have parts that we conceal from others.

However, our hidden self is often perceived as an adversary. "For I do not do the good I want, but the evil I do not want is what I do,"[11] writes Paul as he anguishes over the split he experiences in himself. How does he explain his dilemma? "Now if I do what I do not want, it is no longer I that do it, but sin that dwells within me."[12] Sin is, in such a context, the force that causes us to disown parts of ourselves, that attacks the wholeness of our being. Psychologist C.G. Jung referred to the disowned elements of the self as the "shadow," a fitting name for that which is in the darkened corner of our lives, influencing us, yet remaining hidden from our awareness.

Strange as it may be, our hidden self often surfaces in our relationships with others. It is in our connections with others that we are brought face to face with our shadow; intimate relationships "heighten our awareness of our rough edges."[13]

Marriage therapist and pastoral counselor Harville Hendrix points out three ways that our relationships confront us with the disowned parts of ourselves. First, we are often drawn to others who exhibit qualities that we wish to possess, that we feel are lacking in ourselves.[14] In the story of Donna and Harold, Donna found in Harold her "thinking part"; Harold was drawn to Donna's sensitivity and dependence.

Sometimes complementary matches are quite obvious, even to a casual observer, and they confirm that often quoted axiom that opposites attract. George, a quiet and bespectacled young man, is most comfortable when he is working with his computers. He reads science fiction books for hours. But George is awkward at parties and stutters when he says hello to neighbors; he seems to struggle with any conversation that goes beyond the bounds of computer technology. He marries Jane, a talkative young woman who loves to entertain. Through the years, as he is promoted from job to job in his computer-related occupation, Jane graciously entertains his boss and co-workers, greeting each one warmly, and sends out Christmas cards to a long list of acquaintances and friends.

The second way our relations confront us with ourselves is in the negative traits of others—spouse, friend, lover. They will often have, or appear to have, traits similar to those our parents had; these are the hurtful qualities that caused our childhood wounds. We often deny these attributes during the early phase of a relationship because they conflict with the idealized picture we have of our partner.[15]

Anita, a sad-faced young woman, grew up with a father who was rarely home and an argumentative mother who put Anita in charge of six younger brothers and sisters. Two months after high school graduation, Anita married Doug, a muscular man who was a star athlete. After Anita gave birth to their first child, she had difficulty in immediately losing the extra weight she had gained. Her husband ridiculed her for her heaviness. In the next five years his drinking increased, he often barked orders to Anita about household duties, and he would blow up over small matters. Occasionally, he would slap their son. Anita began taking prescription pills for anxiety. The man she married, in his physical and emotional "absence," was like her rarely present father.

A third way we confront our past is in projecting disowned or denied parts of ourselves into others, much as a movie projector takes an image and shines it onto a blank screen. By attributing negative traits to the other person, we avoid or obscure the parts of ourselves we believe are undesirable.[16] For example, in the scenario above, Anita did not permit herself to accept her anger about her exploitation, abuse, and abandonment, but she connected with her husband, who is quite angry. As long as she stays in the marriage with him, she does not have to acknowledge this forbidden feeling as her own. In fact, she can reassure herself that anger is a dangerous and destructive emotion—as she recognizes it in her husband.

Search for Wholeness

Reviewing the disowned parts of ourselves, outlined above, we begin to see how compelled we are to recreate situations in our present relationships that help in our struggle to complete the unfinished business of our past. As destructive and ineffective as these relationships may be, they demonstrate our drive for wholeness, for completion.

Writer Elizabeth O'Connor has suggested that when Jesus commanded us to love our enemies, he was not only referring to the enemies without, but also to the enemy within. That enemy within is our inner shadow, the part of the self we have learned to disown. Loving the enemy within is acknowledging and accepting our disowned feelings, thoughts, and behavior.

The move to wholeness is promoted through self-acceptance, not self-judgement; through self-forgiveness, not self-condemnation. The poet Robert Bly is prophetic when he says, "The part of you that remains unloved will eventually turn against you." This is not to say we need to approve of all the survival tactics we have learned. In fact, many are self-defeating and even destructive to intimate relationships. But we can appreciate the context out of which such tactics develop, we can learn self-forgiveness, and we can use our new awareness to move toward wholeness.

It is important to know that self-intimacy—loving the enemy within—is the path to intimacy with others. Yet it is in our relationships with others that we are given the opportunity to discover facets of our hidden selves, which we are challenged to love. As psychologist John Welwood observes, "The way we relate to others always reflects the way we relate to parts of ourselves."[17] Therefore, what we look for in others is what we need to discover within ourselves, and what we find displeasing in others often suggests parts of ourselves that we find unacceptable and that we need, at the very least, to learn from.[18]

Consider the situation of Joyce, a social worker in her twenties. She continually complains about her co-worker David, whom she sees as bossy and controlling. When asked by her therapist if there is any part of her that is controlling, Joyce at first becomes defensive. She sees herself as the victim of David's dominating manner. Yet with some gentle probing and humor, she is able to see the controlling part of herself, a part she has found difficult to acknowledge. As time passes, she notices more readily the times when she orders people about, when she wants her own way, and when she likes having her ideas given undivided attention at staff meetings with her colleagues. As she embraces her own behavior, she becomes more tolerant of David's patterns and habits.

The wisdom of Jesus' words is pertinent: "Why do you see the speck in your neighbor's eye, but do not notice the log in your own eye?"[19] We must remove the impediment to our own vision, Jesus suggests, before attempting to remove one from the vision of another. Reowning our projected parts is the only way to see clearly into the eye and heart of another.

But it is not easy to accept and reclaim the disowned parts of ourselves or to acknowledge our learned tactics of survival. When awakening to the ways we have learned to survive by disowning parts of our inner selves, our first response is often shame or guilt. As natural as these may seem initially, they only create an impasse to genuine growth. The fear of judgment is the reason we often keep hidden behind our masks, our persona, even from ourselves.

Speaking Our Truth; Hearing Another's Truth

"Speaking our truth" is a phrase suggested by the profound statement of Paul to his friends in Ephesus, inviting them to speak the truth in love.[20] The phrase is used here to convey that truth is more than a body of teaching or doctrine; it is the truth as it dwells within. Speaking our truth is an invitation to disclose our experience, including our feelings, our thoughts, our hopes, and our dreams. But before we are able to disclose, we must learn to be aware of the hidden self behind the persona.

Joseph Campbell, scholar, writer, and authority on world mythology, in an interview with journalist Bill Moyers, spoke of "following one's bliss," meaning to follow one's deepest longings and inclinations, to live one's truth. To illustrate the negative consequence of not following one's bliss, Joseph Campbell quotes the closing line of Sinclair Lewis's novel *Babbitt*: "I have never done the thing that I wanted to in all my life." "That," said Campbell, "is a man who never followed his bliss."[21] Knowing one's own depth, one's bliss, is self-intimacy.

Knowing one's truth, one's deepest feelings and desires, thoughts and ambitions, is prerequisite to cherishing the truth of another. As we discover and incorporate the disowned parts of ourselves, we become increasingly free to greet the stranger in another. Making these connections, then, is the substance of intimacy.

Chapter Four

Expressions of Intimacy

A basic relationship is not a luxury. It is a basic need.
David Mace

An intimate relationship between people not only asks for mutual openness but also for mutual respectful protection of each other's uniqueness.
Henri J. M. Nouwen

Channels to Intimacy

Vulnerability. Commitment. Honesty. Invariably, such words are among the responses of workshop participants earnestly attempting to untangle the many threads of this curious thing called intimacy.

The words hint at old-fashioned virtues that we intellectually respect. It is another matter, however, for us to introduce these virtues to fit into our daily lives as we are challenged in making important connections with others. How do we show our vulnerability to others in a way that portends strength rather than fragility? Is commitment the same as monogamy, or is monogamy simply one facet of commitment? Do we demand honesty of others while being dishonest with ourselves when it comes to admitting our own needs, feelings, and concerns? The persistence of such questions indicates that for many people intimate relationships have become an arena of confusion, "the new wilderness that brings us face to face with all our gods and demons."[1] Many of the old answers and dictates are no longer adequate to the complexities of building and maintaining personal relationships.

Rainer Maria Rilke, noted earlier (see chapter 1), suggests that we cultivate patience in attempting to love our unsolved questions in life. That seems to be a fitting prescription as we struggle to expand our capacity to make intimate connections. Expanding our capacity for intimacy—emotionally, physically, and spiritually—requires honesty, awareness, sensitivity, silence, and expression. It is these virtues that are channels to the intimate experience.

It is important, however, to distinguish between an intimate moment and an intimate relationship. Most of us have experienced a temporary collapse of the boundaries that separate us from others, a merging into oneness with anther person, with nature, or with the universe. Such moments of connecting can arrive with sexual chemistry, common life suffering, or other shared experiences.

The incident of Jessica McClure, the toddler caught in an abandoned well (see chapter 1), provided a moment of connecting. The townspeople involved in the miraculous rescue felt a deep sense of oneness as they struggled together. Following the rescue of little Jessica, however, much of the intimacy of the crisis dissipated, to be replaced by petty competition and mutual suspicion as the story of the rescue became saleable for a lucrative television movie.

For limited periods of time, however, cultural, ethnic, and religious differences can be transcended by such intimate encounters. Anna is an Amish woman whose membership in her strict religious community is signified by her black bonnet and long purple skirt. Like most people of this Pennsylvania German farming sect, Anna keeps distant from outsiders, especially the "English"—the community's name for anyone who is not Amish—and she stays busy with household chores, her children, and her Bible reading.

Still, on one chilly evening in October, she shared a special moment with Noreen, a sophisticated woman, wife of a stockbroker, and world traveler. Noreen and her husband had hired Anna's husband, a carpenter as well as a farmer, to build a birdhouse on their property; and Anna and her four children had accompanied him to Noreen's.

It was evening as the menfolk turned the headlights of the van to their work site and mixed the concrete that would stabilize the tall post holding the bird house. Noreen shivered with the Amish woman, and her four children huddled nearby, talking about the little birds these shelters would attract. As they glanced at the autumn moon, large, round, and low in the slowly darkening sky, and heard the rustle of the wind, Anna spoke up: "This is like the night my son died." Noreen was startled, as her own son had died painfully of cancer several years before. She found herself asking Anna, "How old was he?"

The Amish woman told how her child had been stricken with a seizure in their garden. Then Noreen told of her son's lingering illness and death. Anna reached for Noreen's hand and spoke again: "Let's go up and meet the moon." Together the women with the children in tow ran up the hill, closer to the moon.

Out of that moment, the two women developed a friendship that is unusual considering the different customs of their two communities. As time has passed, though, Noreen has come to see another side of her friend, a woman who is critical of her husband, and bitter about the loss of a family homestead; a woman who won't talk of change, even of medical progress that would aid ill children in the Amish community. The magical moment that brought them together as grieving mothers has not been repeated since.

Author and psychiatrist M. Scott Peck describes falling in love as a "sudden collapse of a section of an individual's ego boundaries, permitting one to merge his or her identity with that of another person."[2] Such moments, as temporary as they may be, have a powerful impact as we are suddenly released from our aloneness into a convergence with the others or the Other. Many religious experiences are characterized by such an emergence into a reality greater than ourselves.

There are some people whose search for intimacy is confined to trying to create or to duplicate such moments. The intensity of such experiences can become so seductive that normal living seems boring, mundane, and intolerable in comparison. With just such an attitude, Chuck, a man in his forties, complained about his two-year marriage. "We don't have fun together anymore," he murmured. "Things seem so complicated now."

In fact, most people discover a noticeable change after the initial stage in a relationship. Once a commitment is made, a series of hidden expectations emerges, often leading to disillusionment and power struggles. Chuck, however, had gone through a number of brief relationships before his marriage. Each he ended abruptly after a few months. When he met Grace, he felt it was "time to settle down," and since they shared many common interests, she seemed like "a good gamble." But his marriage to Grace confronted Chuck with his difficulty in adjusting to a long-term partnership, a prospect that he had previously successfully avoided.

A closer look at Chuck's background showed that he handled most of the tense situations in his life by withdrawing. Until he was willing to confront his own inner resistance to dealing with his own emotions and those of Grace, he would continue to avoid lasting commitments. The initial moment of intimacy is bound to lead to a time of disappointment. As strong as it may be, an intimate moment is very different from an ongoing intimate relationship.

A relationship requires a sustained commitment to understanding another person, not only with one's mind but also with one's heart. It means appreciating differences and tolerating times of boredom and lessening interest, desert periods of diminished emotion. It involves skills of identifying, expressing, and containing feelings as well as sharing support and nurturing, establishing the boundaries between the "I" and the "we." It requires creating a safety zone where the other person can come without fear of judgment and criticism so that feelings, thoughts, hopes, and fears can be freely exchanged.

Emotional Intimacy

Most definitions of intimacy offer or imply some reference to the disclosure of feelings. Expressing one's anger, sadness, fear, and joy in relating to others is an essential part of creating an intimate connection. Emotions are the inner link with one's core self, and a mutual interchange of feeling is a way of connecting with the inner being of another.

Molly, a workshop participant, described a time of emotional intimacy that occurred while she was hospitalized after a life-threatening automobile accident. She recalled her tremendous anxiety as she became aware of her severe injuries, several fractured ribs, a broken collarbone, a concussion, internal traumas, and many painful bruises. She also felt lonely, because she was separated from her elderly parents, who lived several hundred miles away, and from her only brother, Jon, who was stationed with the Army in Germany.

Molly had recently transferred to a new job in a new community. The few friends she had made since then sent get-well cards, and two co-workers visited her in the hospital. But is was a hospital nurse, Norma, who became her lifeline during this time of crisis. Norma, sensing Molly's isolation and despair, would spend a few minutes each day talking with her, even if it required staying beyond the end of her shift. At first, their conversations focused on Molly's family and work, and gradually on her fears and loneliness. Norma would gently inquire and attentively listen as Molly talked about her concerns, frustrations, and impatience with the healing process.

It was clear to both women that these discussions were not mutual. Norma remained the professional and Molly the patient, yet Molly felt understood, accepted, and nurtured in ways she had not experienced before. Norma's concern and compassion were obviously genuine. To Norma, Molly was a "thou" not an "it." Molly's eyes filled with tears as she described the impact of Norma's presence on her life during her recovery.

It was shortly before Molly was discharged from the hospital, however, that their relationship entered a deeper level of intimacy. Molly discovered by talking with another nurse that Norma's son had been killed in an automobile collision just six months before Molly's accident. Molly was overwhelmed with grief for Norma's loss and felt guilty for adding to Norma's personal burden. Molly wondered how Norma could listen so attentively to her when Norma herself was in such pain. But Molly also acknowledged some personal anger that Norma had not spoken about this part of her life, that she had not shared her own loss.

In Molly's eyes their conversations seemed very one-sided. Molly was certainly a "thou" to Norma, but their relationship was not an I-Thou" partnership, since Molly knew very little about Norma's struggles, feelings, and concerns.

The evening after Molly discovered Norma's tragedy, Norma arrived for their usual conversation. But Molly confronted Norma with her new knowledge. "Why didn't you choose to tell me about your son's death?" she asked, showing some disappointment and irritation. Norma did not answer immediately. She meditated on her response for what seemed to Molly a long time. Finally, Norma said,

"I'm not sure of all my reasons for not talking about my situation. But I know it seemed important to withhold my own grief to give you space to speak about your pain, and it seemed intrusive and unprofessional for me to share my experience with you."

Molly's irritation was mixed with and then replaced by appreciation as she recognized Norma's determination to be present with her during her recovery. "But now I am feeling different, and our relationship has changed," Norma continued. "I now see you as a friend, not as a patient, and I have experienced some healing through listening to you." Then as she spoke about her son's death, her eyes filled with tears. From that moment of intimate connecting, Norma and Molly established an ongoing, genuine friendship that they have maintained for five years.

It took courage for Molly to confront Norma with the lack of mutuality in their relationship. Her confrontation opened the way for the two women to share significant feelings with each other, touching the innermost core of each other's lives. The intimacy that evolved between them required a new level of mutual openness. An "I-Thou" relationship, a deep inner connection from being to being, is formed only when both persons disclose and listen, attend and empathize. Psychologist and author John Welwood calls such a meeting a "soul-connection," an engagement that amplifies and enriches the qualities of each person involved.[3]

One of the barriers to building such a soul connection is the difficulty we sometimes have in identifying our feelings. In every family, as we have seen, certain feelings are recognized and expressed; others are denied and concealed. We may recognize our anger, for example, yet be unaware of sadness; or identify our sadness, but deny our fear. Often familiar feelings are used to cover less acceptable feelings. Anger, for example, is a frequent mask for fear. Identifying our hidden feelings is not easy. We may anticipate being criticized for forbidden feelings, feelings we have learned to deny.

Recognizing our feelings, however, presents us with a predicament. It is a dilemma well defined in the words of the writer of Ecclesiastes: "a time to keep silence, and a time to speak." Keeping silence or speaking out, in other words, containment or expression, are alternatives that need to be balanced as we relate to others.

Possibly one of the most threatening feelings is the feeling of anger. Most of us have little real instruction in dealing constructively with it. When we are able to admit our sadness, tears can readily spill out. When we recognize our joy, we can spontaneously express it with laughing, shouting, or giggling. But anger is another story. Distorted anger expressed irresponsibly can be threatening or hurtful to others as well as ourselves, and we need to understand ways of handling it.

Gordon and Barbara's story illustrates the necessity for the containment and expression of anger. It became apparent in the first counseling session that Gordon dominated the relationship with his pervasive anger. Several times he impulsively vented his anger at Barbara, who would visibly draw back much like a scolded child. Efforts by the counselor to support Barbara in expressing her opinion to her husband proved useless. Either Barbara would act confused and self-effacing or Gordon would pounce on her and contradict her views.

In such a situation, it is important for a third party to avoid casting the dominating partner as a persecutor and the eclipsed partner as the victim. In that scenario, the counselor would be then tempted to become the rescuer, completing the circle to the detriment of all.[4] Through confrontation, Gordon would not be convinced of his dominating behavior, nor would Barbara become more expressive through sympathy.

A breakthrough occurred in the middle of the sixth session when Gordon broke into tears as he remembered an incident from his childhood. Gordon recalled a day when he was just seven years old. He had stood on the sidewalk in front of his home and watched as his mother was being driven away to be hospitalized for severe depression. He saw the car become smaller against the horizon, and he felt his own smallness, fear, and helplessness. He recalled how his father in the following months gradually withdrew into his work and into silence, seldom speaking to his three children. As Gordon told this childhood memory, he seemed very vulnerable. He was embarrassed by his crying, by what he termed his weakness and loss of control.

At first, Barbara recoiled from Gordon's grief, almost as alarmed by his tears as she was terrified of his anger. Yet this show of need evoked Barbara's empathy, and she reached to hold her husband's hand. Slowly during the weeks that followed, Gordon was able to treat his sadness with less self-recrimination and to accept the frightened little boy who still lived behind his protective anger. Gordon also became more willing to contain his feelings so that Barbara would have an opportunity to express some of her own anger and frustration.

Another client, Marty, had great difficulty in acknowledging her tremendous anger toward her mother. Marty described her mother as neurotic and perfectionistic, but would always add that she couldn't bring herself to blame her mother for her shortcomings. Despite assurances that giving voice to one's experience is quite different from blaming someone, Marty continued to fear and avoid her anger. Even when she intellectually recognized that she had reasons to feel angry about her mother's mistreatment of her, Marty remained inhibited, saying that she was not ready to express her feelings.

Only when the counselor permitted Marty not to express her anger was she able to free herself to experience the anger itself. Then she could express it indirectly; she refused to attend the large Thanksgiving dinner orchestrated by her mother. As months passed, Marty continued to give voice to those uncomfortable feelings by complaining in the therapy room about her mother's behavior, and by journalizing an imaginary dialogue with her mother in which she told her mother of her anger. The small steps in the process were important to Marty because as a child when Marty had become angry, her mother had threatened to abandon her.

With the growth of the human potential movement and the prevalence of self-help books in the past two decades, many people mistakenly believe that to hold back in expressing feelings makes one emotionally unhealthy and that it is healthy to express feelings at all times. But containment, or keeping silence, offers another important option. Containment is not necessarily a denial of what we feel, nor is it an avoidance of the risk of expressing our feelings. Rather, containment creates the space we need to learn what our feelings have to teach us so that we may have clarity in expressing them effectively. Almost always there are feelings other than the ones we are initially aware of. We need to know these. Too, we don't have a right to express feelings that are abusive to others and do harm to them. Containment is a way of learning more about ourselves and also of not overwhelming a partner, friend, or associate.

Larry, a recovering alcoholic and drug addict, is beginning to explore in therapy his own family of origin. It includes an alcoholic father, who criticized him harshly and beat him physically, and a mother unable to protect Larry. Because she was also incapable of addressing or validating Larry's anger about his unhappy family life, his mother sent him to a reform school at fourteen. There he was again abused and humiliated, this time by his peers.

Larry dealt with his feelings of pain and anger by hiding them in drugs and alcohol. His life grew increasingly out of control until he became involved in self-help groups and therapy. But five years into recovery, Larry remains an angry man. He snaps at his children, shouts at his wife, and fears that he will one day repeat his father's pattern and strike them. Because he has been working hard in therapy, Larry knows intellectually that the anger covers the hurt and pain of his unhappy childhood, and he blames himself for not being able to cry in front of others.

"I wish I could cry like her," he says, indicating another group member, a woman, who easily becomes tearful when talking about her childhood. He then criticizes himself for not "doing therapy right." Unfortunately, Larry is attempting to escape his anger by focusing on other feelings that he thought he should be feeling.

It was important that Larry be validated in his anger and learn to accept his angry feelings. He had every right to feel anger because of the abuse, emotional neglect, and parental abandonment that he suffered during his childhood and young adult years. But he also needed to learn two things: to recognize the cues that signaled his anger—name calling, profanity, flushed skin, and shallow breathing—and to own his anger in safe places. These included the counseling room, so that his anger did not splash out at his wife and children. Once Larry was able to release his anger in therapy and feel the support of his group, he was able to cry, to express his grief and pain for his unmet needs, loneliness, and loss. By learning to recognize and release the old anger safely, Larry was eventually able to express his current anger in manageable ways to his wife, without yelling or using abusive language.

When we are angry or hurt or sad, we need to ask how we can express our feelings in a way that will enhance the relationship, rather than diminish it. As Gordon, the dominant husband, gave himself permission to explore his anger rather than discharge it indiscriminately, he began to understand the fear of abandonment that was underneath his need to dominate. This disowned fear would have remained hidden for as long as he persisted in focusing on controlling those outside of himself.

Therapist Harville Hendrix has pointed out that many times, repetitive, emotional criticisms of a partner may be a reflection of one's own unmet needs and disowned parts.[5] Much of Gordon's criticism of Barbara, for instance, covered his own fear of losing her support and of facing his own vulnerability. As he was able to accept this new knowledge of his hidden self and become more whole, he was also able to accept the previously unacceptable parts of Barbara's personality that he had so frequently criticized.

An intimate relationship accommodates the stranger in ourselves and in the other. It gives us and others the space and permission to feel what we feel, to think what we think.[6] In the story of Norma and Molly in the hospital, Norma's attentive listening, empathetic understanding, and willingness to contain her own emotions in order to give space and attention to Molly were essential to Molly's healing.

Yet creating a free space where people can arrive undisturbed is rare. We are schooled in dualistic thinking that specializes in finding fault and placing blame. We internalize critical voices that divide feelings and opinions into right and wrong. We develop mind-sets that do not tolerate ambiguity. Even the dictionary uses words like "uncertainty" and "vagueness" to define ambiguity. Yet the term also conveys a willingness to accommodate a diversity of feeling and thought, of opinions and views. Accommodation to what is in us and others does not mean we need to like what we feel or agree with another's views. It does mean that we approach ourselves and others with an attitude of learning and understanding, rather than judgment and criticism.

Therapists Jordan and Margaret Paul have suggested we "accept the fact that all of us always have very good, respectable, important, and appropriate reasons for feeling and behaving as we do."[7] Making this assumption helps us understand that fears underlie our own and others' behavior. [8]

Gender and Intimacy

Applying the assumption that there are good, respectable, important, and appropriate reasons for our feeling and behaving as we do is particularly crucial when facing the differences in the way men and women deal with feelings. Although the area of female-male emotional distinctions is complex and difficult to discuss, the differences are clearly evident in the therapy setting and in conversations between couples. Writer and psychologist Lillian Rubin states the difference this way:

> Stop a woman in mid-sentence with the question, "What are you feeling right now?" and you might have to wait a bit while she reruns the mental tape to capture the moment just passed. . . . But, more than likely, she'll think for a while and come up with an answer. The same is not true of a man. For him, a similar question usually will bring a sense of wonderment that one would even ask it, followed quickly by an uncomprehending and puzzled response. "What do you mean?" he'll ask. "I was just talking," he'll say.[9]

This comparative approach to understanding the ways men and women deal with emotions can perhaps lead to greater empathy and appreciation of gender differences. There is no doubt that generally men have integrated well the lessons of childhood that teach the denial of feelings or the camouflaging of them under a calm exterior of rationality.[10] Yet like many stereotypes this explanation of male emotion conceals as much as it illuminates. There are many men aware and expressive of their feelings and many women as closed to emotion as the most unexpressive male. It is important, therefore, to avoid attaching simplistic labels onto particular modes of feeling and perception.[11] Writer Sam Keen reminds us:

> Good men and women alike can be characterized as compassionate, aggressive, nurturing, powerful, intuitive, reasonable, playful, wise, erotic, or loyal. . . . Likewise men and women share equally in the capacity for greed, cruelty, violence, and the desire to dominate those who are less powerful than themselves.[12]

Yet there are few arenas that cause more confusion and defensiveness, or create more barriers to emotional intimacy, than gender differences. Nor is there any arena that requires more tolerance and understanding.

Few of Fred's friends would describe him as a highly emotional man. Controlled and quick-witted, he is socially adept, rarely at a loss for words during conversations, and he often lightens unpleasant situations with an anecdote or joke. But Fred also is a sensitive man who is quite able to connect to the emotional states of others. He enjoys a wide circle of men friends, dating back to his high school and college years. Recently, Natalie, the twenty-two-year-old daughter of a man who was Fred's fraternity brother, contacted Fred. Her father had died in the Vietnam War shortly before she was born, and she was seeking information about him, as her mother rarely talked about her late husband.

What Natalie requested was a letter detailing any small particles of information: her father's favorite food, the color of his eyes, what his dreams and ambitions had been. Since her father was one of Fred's closest friends, Fred wrote several pages of recollection of this special man and contacted several of his fraternity brothers throughout the country, asking each to contribute a memory. As Fred talks about this project, he does not discuss feelings directly, but it is apparent that his regard and feeling for this special man is genuine and deep and that this man's early death was a grievous loss of friendship, presence, and exceptional potential.

Emotional Triangles

In growing in our capacity for intimacy, we are wise to be aware of the problems caused by emotional triangles. An emotional triangle has been defined as "an ongoing, repetitive cycle of interactions that involves three people."[13] Triangles can be used as a means to incur distance in a relationship or to create a pretext for closeness. "Triangling" is a means of keeping a safe distance, a way of avoiding painful—what may be seen as unsolvable—problems in a partnership. It permits two people to divert from the intensity of their relationship by involving a third party in their undeclared and unacknowledged conflict. The third party can be a child, a lover, or even a job.

A common and easily recognized form of triangling that tends to produce a pseudo closeness is gossip. Gloria, a group therapy participant, tells of her repetitive conversations with her mother, Eva. Their recurring complaint sessions would focus either on her father or on her younger sister, who was in constant conflict with the mother. During one of these conversations it dawned on Gloria that she and her mother never spoke about each other. Concentrating the discussion on the other family members permitted Gloria and Eva to avoid the far more difficult subject of their own relationship. For the mother and daughter, their talks reinforced a pseudo closeness, which helped camouflage the lack of genuine intimacy that, ideally, would center on their own feelings, needs hopes and frustrations. Gloria also acknowledged that these mother-daughter sessions increased the distance between her and her father, who was the focus of much of her mother's frustration and complaints. In the therapy group, Gloria began to be alert to her own anger, a reaction to her mother's constant invitations to join her in opposing her father. Finally, in an act that took enormous courage and support by other members of the group, Gloria changed her stance with her mother. Instead of participating in the criticism of her father and sister, Gloria maintained a detached concern. She listened carefully and silently as Eva initiated the ritualistic dialogue of familiar complaints. Gloria could feel her anger growing as the conversation followed its predictable course. But she contained her anger and slowly focused the conversation toward herself and her mother. Each of Gloria's efforts met with her mother's sarcasm and criticism. Eventually, Gloria suggested to her mother that she and her father consider talking to someone who could help them sort through their painful differences. Eve responded with irritation and defensiveness, but Gloria did not react to her mother with anger, but rather with determination and concern. Gloria stayed emotionally connected with Eva and affirmed the significance and seriousness of her mother's complaints. She did not, however, join in the criticism of her father. Gloria also expressed her desire that her mother find some peace and enjoyment in her life.

Over a period of time a more genuine sharing of feeling between Gloria and Eva emerged. This deeper level of relating could not have occurred as long as the two women had remained in the grips of the triangle of mutual complaint. However, a stance of detached concern is not easily established. We cannot control the emotional reactions of other people, but we can be responsible for our own emotional attitude and response. As we stop focusing on changing others and take responsibility for our own feelings and behavior, we feel an enormous release of energy.

Moving out of a triangle, as the above story illustrates, is a difficult and sometimes painful process. The three participants will often increase their efforts to maintain the triangle. The alternatives to a triangled situation are frequently seen as angry withdrawal or enmeshed participation. The attitude of detached concern, with which Gloria engaged her mother, is one that preserves an appropriate distance while maintaining the emotional connection of caring.

Although triangling may provide a temporary reprieve from a tense, even unbearable, situation, it does not promote the mutual regard essential to intimacy. It is impossible to avoid becoming a part of triangles in relating to others. Third parties, both real and imaginary, are brought into relationships on a regular basis. However, we can significantly move toward deeper intimacy when we recognize our own particular triangling tendencies and ask ourselves what fear or pain we are avoiding by staying within the crucible of the triangle.

Other Intimate Connections

In our search for intimacy we are helped by knowing that intimacy, happily, can be enjoyed in varied ways. Authors Howard and Charlotte Clinebell identify several kinds of intimacy.[14] Most relationships will not embrace every kind, and some will contain only a few. Among the intimate connections identified by the Clinebells and others are intellectual intimacy, the exchange of ideas and opinions; aesthetic intimacy, the sharing of experiences of wonder and beauty such as nature, music, or art; and play intimacy, spontaneous fun-loving activity regardless of age.

We have also noted crisis intimacy, which can come with facing a tragedy with others. Watching the kind of closeness and support that can develop in the midst of an earthquake, for example, can inspire our deepest admiration. But a particular crisis may not come from an outside catastrophic event. It may come from a relationship itself as partners face their differences or confront the pain of betrayal or disappointment.

In less dramatic ways, there is the closeness that can come from sharing significant tasks, such as participating in a musical production or play, a community reforestation project, or the building of a house. Todd and Clair discovered their greatest closeness when they planned and built their first home. They spent hours working through the details of the blueprints and learning construction skills. They labored evenings and weekends on specific projects, meticulously attending to details. Todd, reflecting on the experience, said, "It was demanding and exhausting at times, but we never felt closer."

Still another way we connect is through creative effort. The product of such creativity can take many forms, a drama perhaps or a musical. But the product need not be so aesthetic or concrete. The shape the creativity takes may be the raising of children or encouraging of the gifts and talents of others. Teaching can be a creative act of forming the minds and intellects of the young and the not so young. The specific result is not the focus here, but rather the process of generating, producing, and creating. Psychologist Erik Erikson designates "generativity versus stagnation" as one of the eight stages of human development. Although generativity "is primarily the concern in establishing and guiding the next generation,"[15] it can also be expressed in other acts of care and encouragement. Consider the relationship between a mentor and a student. Each brings something to the interaction: The mentor, experience and insight; the student, curiosity and respect. Creativity can also take the form of "co-creation" of one another, helping a spouse grow into his or her potentialities in the context of a committed relationship.[16]

It is apparent, then, that there are many ways people can come together. Even people who are fundamentally incompatible can share experiences of intimacy. Some expressions of intimacy can be the beginning of a deeper connection. But often such intimate occasions are time-limited and dependent on the conditions that draw the people together. The people's relationship can easily revert into periods of tension and conflict when circumstances change. For example, Todd and Clair, whose story we started above, grew close while building their house, but they soon found themselves distressed after the task was completed. The time and interest vacuum created by the completion of their dream house quickly filled with bickering and disappointment as they faced the lack of emotional intimacy between them.

Yet the possibility of relapses should not keep us from appreciating the power of intimate occasions. They can break through to our consciousness the potential for deeper ways of connecting with others and with the universe. Such events can provide the motivation for the commitment necessary for a sustained intimate relationship. And out of the resonance that comes with opening up to deeper layers of feeling and thought can come a further commitment to a mutual unveiling of the core of our lives to one another.

Physical and Sexual Intimacy

We first experience intimacy not with words but with touch. The organ of the skin is our first link in life, with our parents, caregivers, and others, as we move from the protective womb into the uncertain world of relationships. We sense trust by how firmly and securely we are held; we accept love through the warmth, tenderness, and gentleness of touch. Author Eric Berne used the word *stroking* to convey the fundamental importance of physical touch as prerequisite to verbal affection. Without sufficient touch we cannot survive, but with inappropriate or violent touch we can become wounded in ways that affect us throughout our lives.

Our willingness to touch and be touched, like other forms of human interaction, stems from the experiences and messages of childhood. There are many families where physical contact is avoided. Lee came from such a family. In remembering family interactions, Lee recalled that his mother stopped cuddling him when he reached kindergarten age. He could not recall being hugged or touched by his father, except for handshakes following graduations. He did not remember seeing his parents holding or caressing one another. Even in times of sadness or loss, family members withdraw in silence rather than stay close to one another or comfort each other with touch. So when Lee met Mariam, it was strange, refreshing, and a bit unsettling to be with someone who freely hugged him and held hands. Reluctantly, Lee responded but soon found himself withdrawing. He felt sadness, guilt, and anger at himself for being unable to reach out, to spontaneously hold Mariam. He felt like a prisoner in his own body.

To his credit, Lee recognized his discomfort with physical contact as a limitation he wanted to change. He did not rationalize his problem or place blame on Mariam for being too physical. In counseling sessions, after he and Mariam had spoken freely about his discomfort in making physical contact, they decided to take dance lessons. Dancing would be a natural way to ease Lee into physical contact. Lee also brought himself to situations, including a workshop, where touching other people was safely and respectfully demonstrated. He faced, rather than avoided, his uneasiness. In this way he is becoming progressively more freed from his emotional prison.

Sexual intimacy is more than a physical act—an obvious truth. Yet in a culture that exploits sex to sell everything from toothpaste to automobiles, where lovemaking is abbreviated to "making it," and emphasis is often on "good technique," we need reminding that sexual intimacy is the interaction of whole persons. In the words of D. H. Lawrence, "Sex . . . means the whole of the relationship between man and woman. And the relation of man to woman is wide as all life."[17]

The ebb and flow of sexual intimacy involves emotional honesty and direct communication as well as physical contact. Many complaints a counselor hears regarding sex, reflected in such statements as "He seems totally unaware of what I feel" or "Sometimes I just want to be held," are pleas to be acknowledged as whole persons. Sexual intimacy like other expressions of intimacy, requires a respect for the "I" of each individual as well as the coming together as a "we." When one partner feels exploited or used, the "I" of the relationship is eclipsed and sexual intimacy is diminished.

There are times when sexual feelings also demand to be contained if we want to experience fully the joys of sexual intimacy. As with anger, it is important to discern when the power of sexual desire must be kept silent before it finds expression. Too often, a person will identify a feeling of attraction as mutual, and take that identification as license to plunge ahead into a physical relationship without first examining important relational questions. Does this other person have a sense of himself or herself? How deep is his self-knowledge? Is she able to identify a variety of feelings and make responsible choices about their expression? Does he have the ability to hear others when they speak on an emotional level and respect their revelations? Does she have the ability to make and keep commitments? Is he a person who can be intimate and connected?

Containment—acknowledging sexual feelings but choosing to experience them without acting immediately on them—gives us time to examine honestly the experience of our relationship with a person. Only by bracketing the feelings can we reflect on the question. Then we may be able to move from the containment of the sexual feelings to their expression, trusting that the risks that we take at this point are based on health and actual potential for relatedness.

Spiritual Intimacy

In our great search for relatedness, we are forced beyond the confines of human intervention. In the words of Howard and Charlotte Clinebell: "In the fullest expression of intimacy there is a vertical dimension, a sense of relatedness to the universe."[18] When the biblical author of John writes "let us love one another, because love is from God; everyone who loves is born of God and knows God. Whoever does not love does not know God, for God is love,"[19] we are being reminded that the unifying force of our lives and the universe is love.

Spiritual intimacy is our relationship to the divine source of love that transcends as well as infiltrates our love. It is this experience of spiritual relatedness that is the origin of our oneness with each other. Again in spiritual intimacy we experience the separateness of One who is apart from and greater than ourselves, yet is together with us, as close as our heart beat.

Chapter Five

Making Life Connections

The human encounter depends on an inner connection. To be in touch with you I need to be in touch within.
James Hillman

When you can be in your own personal space while you are also in the same space you share with another, you are being intimate.
Thomas and Patrick Malone

Healthy Self-Love

    A healthy sense of love for ourselves is the foundation for intimacy with others. But what does it mean to really love oneself? The word *self-loving* has often been misinterpreted to suggest selfishness, arrogance, and sinful pride. Even the late twentieth-century tradition of self-help books and tapes, which offers prescriptions for affirming goodness and humanness, often provide incomplete direction because they suggest that affirmative statements are the only way we show ourselves that we love ourselves.
    Although affirmative statements can be extremely helpful in building self-esteem, they are just one component, it is important to note, of healthy self-love. What we love is what we designate as precious—and we offer gentleness, tenderness, and attention accordingly. A caring parent, for instance, will treat a new infant with attentiveness, listening to every small nuance of its being, accepting each sigh, whimper, and gurgle as an important communication. A caring parent also will attend to cries for nourishment,

rest, and contact with others by creating an environment that is nurturing, comfortable, and safe. With this attention, the parent accepts the vulnerable and needy aspects of the child, aspects that may prove from the adult's perspective demanding and even inconvenient.

We trust in the intrinsic value of what we love. We care for what we value. "Love is," in the words of psychologist Erich Fromm, "the active concern for the life and the growth of that which we love."[1] Or as defined by psychiatrist M. Scott Peck, love is "the will to extend one's self for the purpose of nurturing one's own or another's spiritual growth."[2] Too often, though, we do not show active concern or extend nurture to ourselves when our own needs come begging for our attention.

We can speak of intimacy as embracing the dimensions of the intrapersonal, connecting to our inner self; the interpersonal, relating to other persons and the created order; and the transpersonal, our relationship to the Source of life, to the Infinite. But in reality, the experience of intimacy cannot be separated so neatly. We know our inner selves only in community with other persons, and our capacity for I-Thou relationships with others reveals our fundamental relationships with the One who underlies all our relating. In the words of philosopher and theologian Martin Buber: "Every particular *Thou* is a glimpse through to the eternal *Thou*."[3]

The close interaction of these three dimensions of intimacy (intrapersonal, interpersonal, and transpersonal) is brought out in Jesus' familiar words, "You shall love the Lord your God with all your heart, and with all your soul, and with all your mind, and with all your strength.... 'You shall love your neighbor as yourself.'"[4] This great commandment of love carries profound insight into the dynamics of intimacy. It clearly implies that love for our neighbor is based on a healthy love of self. In the words of writer and Jungian analyst James Hillman, which we quoted at the beginning of the chapter, "To be in touch with you I need to be in touch within."[5] Although self-love is popularly equated with selfishness, in fact, as Erich Fromm points out, "selfish persons are incapable of loving others, but they are not capable of loving themselves either."[6]

Healthy self-love is based on our experiences of being respected, nurtured, and attended to as we grow from childhood into adulthood. Our need for attentive care never ceases, but our infant experience of "original wholeness"—that is, of the idyllic existence in the womb and during the first few months of life, when our physical needs are cared for immediately—provides us with an image of our unity and connectedness with the universe. Our experiences of being touched, fed, and cared for through the years are integrated and crystallized into our conclusion "I am loved."[7] Of course, this ideal unity with our world is challenged by the reality of disappointment and the inevitable wounds from the lack of responsiveness of our caretakers. And each stage of our growth brings new areas of potential wounding.[8] Despite the disillusionment we inescapably experience as we face the conditions and limits on the love we are given, we continue to retain a sense of our basic wholeness and of our grounding in unconditional love.

The search for our original wholeness can lead us to unrealistic expectations of others. Therapist Harville Hendrix observes that when we enter marriage, we often bring the expectation that our partner will "magically restore this feeling of wholeness."[9] Such expectations are certain to bring disappointment in relationships with others, but the search can eventually steer us to the awareness that the essential foundation of our life, the force that unifies, is the One whose nature is love. "God is love, and those who abide in love abide in God, and God abides in them."[10] When we realize that there is One whose love for us is unconditional, we have the confidence to say, "I am loved; therefore, I am lovable." Knowing we are loved opens the door to making connection with the deep, inner self that begins to emerge in an atmosphere of acceptance.

Making Connection with Oneself

Writer and physician Paul Tournier reminds us that there remains in every person, even for one's self, something of an impenetrable mystery.[11] We are not, like characters in many a novel, film, or play, finished products of a writer's imagination. Life constantly challenges us to grow and unfold, although at times we may resist this process of becoming and stubbornly cling to familiar perceptions of ourselves and others. The inner reality of ourselves and of others is clothed in the mysterious, often concealed behind the persona, that outer self that we reveal to others.

How do we confront the mysterious in ourselves and in others? According to philosopher and theologian Sam Keen, "we approach the mystery of our being by respectfully listening, by recollecting our experience, by cherishing paradox, and, above all, by loving what we cannot reduce to understanding."[12] These four steps can be used as our path to self-intimacy, to encountering the mystery of our inner, hidden self.

Listening

In a world where rival voices vie for our attention and loyalty, listening has become difficult and confusing. By developing a protective mentality that filters the multitude of voices, we learn to protect ourselves from being overwhelmed by messages telling us how to dress, what to eat, and how to think. Yet subtly and ironically, this protective armor also may cause us to lose contact with our own innermost voices and not trust them. Increasingly, then, we are persuaded that the answers lie outside ourselves as we go from authority to authority, from book to book, in a never-ending search for the "right" counsel and advice.

Commonly heard when people come to therapy is the request "Tell me what to do?" Many clients seem to assume that another person's solution will allow them to feel as if they are whole persons again, that they can return to the comfort they enjoyed before their vexing problems surfaced. Tony is someone who entered therapy with such a fix-it attitude. In response to the question "What brings you to see me?" Tony proceeded to outline a complex job situation involving Howard, a friend and colleague, with whom he has worked for a number of years. He described one particular incident in which Howard made key decisions regarding a work project without consulting Tony. The decisions later proved embarrassing, and both men were criticized by their supervisor.

Tony recalled how he stood mute before his boss, listening to the harsh words, waiting for Howard to step forward to take the blame, wanting desperately to speak in his own defense, yet being unable to utter a word. After recounting this emotional episode, Tony asked, "What should I say to Howard?"

"What do you want to say to Howard?"

"I don't know! I thought you could tell me the best thing to say," Tony almost pleaded.

"Well, as a matter of fact, Tony, I cannot tell you what you should say to Howard. It depends on what you feel, what you want from him, and even how important the relationship is to you."

Tony looked confused. He had "climbed the mountain" to get the word, the "right" thing to say, but instead he was faced with a guru with more questions than answers.

"Perhaps you could give me some hints on things to say," Tony persisted, as though the therapist were holding out on him, and perhaps hoping that lessening the request to a "hint" would bring forth the sought-after advice.

"Tell me, Tony, what was happening inside of you as you stood with Howard listening to your boss's words?" the therapist asked, ignoring Tony's last effort to pry out an answer.

Tony, looking a little startled, replied, "Confused, I guess."

"Mad, sad, glad, or afraid—those are some of your choices," the therapist said playfully.

"Mad, I guess," Tony answered. And with his answer Tony began a journey inward, an excursion into his feelings.

In fact, Tony's feelings were present and being expressed all along, although partly blocked from his awareness. Following the job incident, Tony had distanced himself from Howard, returning only perfunctory answers to his friend's effort to initiate conversation. Although Howard had apologized for his conduct, Tony believed Howard did not fully understand the event nor take it seriously. Yet it was Tony who avoided facing the seriousness of the episode for himself by focusing on what he should say to Howard. The experience with Howard raised for Tony long-forgotten memories of betrayal from his childhood. Painful memory fragments formed the context of Tony's inner experience of the incident with Howard. There was a hidden self Tony was ignoring.

One humorous event demonstrates the distortion of looking outward as a way of avoiding the inward. I was sitting in my car at a red traffic light about six feet behind another car. We were on slight grade, so I pulled the emergency brake as I waited for the light to change. The car ahead began to drift slowly backward toward me, and I noticed that the woman in the driver's seat was looking intensely in her rearview mirror and frantically waving her hand—or was it a fist? In some panic I hit the horn as I saw her car moving even more rapidly toward mine. Suddenly the cars bumped, and we both were out of our cars in a flash, she a bit more quickly than I. Irritated, she said, "Don't you have brakes on that car!"

"What do you mean?" I said (calmly of course). "You drifted into me!"

Fortunately, she realized what had happened. She had been so focused on my car in the mirror that she did not realize her own foot was lifting from the brake pedal. No damage was done. We saw the humor in the incident, and we left a little wiser for it.

Sometimes we can get stuck in looking into the rearview mirror, focusing on the behavior of others while ignoring what is happening within ourselves. The story of Tony extends this common truth. Tony kept looking to those outside himself to define who he was and who he was to be. His insistence on getting an answer to his problem of what to say to his colleague reveals his much deeper distrust of his own insights, feelings, and ability to think clearly. When Tony came to the counselor, he was not seeking information or support in defining his own feelings and wants. Rather, he was looking to some authority who would define for him what he should do, and even more important, what he should be.

In the book *The Art of Intimacy*, psychiatrists Patrick and Thomas Malone have stated well the dilemma of the fix-it approach: "You cannot be advised into *selfhood*, you cannot be 'told' who you are. There is no list of things you can *do* to *make* yourself *be* more naturally who you are."[13] We can learn to speak our thoughts, feelings, and wants more decisively. But we cannot be taught how we feel. Patrick and Thomas Malone point out that "feeling is a natural response. We can no more teach sadness, tenderness, sexuality, anger, or empathy than we can teach the complex intricacies of cardiac rhythm regulation, or body fluid electrolyte balances."[14] What is said here of feeling is also true for our deepest thoughts, insights, and wants. These also are not teachable, but they are learnable. "Whereas one teaches what is not known, one learns by making conscious what is already naturally known."[15]

Intimacy is not just presenting ourselves differently; it is developing ourselves as whole and connected persons. Such an experience of being cannot be taught, but it can be discovered as we connect with our inner feelings, insights, wants, and thoughts.

It is important to note that Tony's fix-it approach is not confined to those seeking help. Sometimes it can be found in the mind-set of the helper, particularly helping professionals who are often asked for advice and frequently may feel compelled to "do" something for the person seeking their assistance. Yet yielding to the temptation to advise others, that is, rescue them from their struggles, makes them an extension of ourselves and not a person in their own right.[16] It takes a counselor with a deep respect for another, whether a child, a client, a spouse, or a friend, to be present without being anxious, to listen without advising, to invite a different perspective without conveying obligation.

The story of the rich young man who comes to Jesus with the question "Teacher, what good deed must I do to have eternal life?" provides excellent insight into Jesus' approach to the fix-it mentality. The man is obviously seeking the ultimate answer to salvation, but Jesus does not give it to him. Instead Jesus challenges the young man's action of seeking one more authority to tell him what to do. Jesus questions him: "Why do you ask me about what is good?" and then reminds the man to keep the commandments.

"Which ones?" the man asks.

When Jesus outlines a few, the young man responds, "I have kept all these," and, much like Tony, he persists, "What do I still lack?"

The response of Jesus rocks the man to his core: "If you wish to be perfect, go, sell your possessions, and give the money to the poor, and you will have treasure in heaven; then come, follow me."[17] On the surface, this response sounds like a directive, but, in fact, Jesus summons the man to confront what it is that blocks his movement to the inner experience of eternal life, to having "treasure in heaven." In doing this Jesus shows that this treasure is not confined to the future, but is a part of being a complete person in the present.[18]

The congruence of doing and being is an essential prerequisite to becoming intimate. It is only when our inner being is congruent with our outer doing that we are able to relate to others with integrity. In a culture that continually focused on external commandments and prescribed behavior, Jesus' teachings emphasized this congruence. His criticism of the Pharisees and other fundamentalist religious groups of his day was that they were hypocrites, those who play acted by following the right behavior but neglected their inner beings. He compared them to whitewashed tombs, beautiful on the outside, but inside full of dead men's bones.[19] Jesus used strong words to confront the lack of integrity of these religiously righteous people. He put correct behavior in right relationship to a compassionate heart.

Essential to self-intimacy is knowing one's own heart, one's deepest feelings and necessities. A young poet sent some of his poems to the famous poet Rainer Maria Rilke. He asked Rilke if his poetry was good. In response Rilke wrote:

> You ask me whether your verses are good. You ask me. You have asked others before. You send them to magazines. You compare them with other poems. . . . Now . . . I beg you give up all that. You are looking outward. . . . Nobody can counsel and help you, nobody. There is only one single way. Go into yourself. Search for the reason that bids you write; find out whether it is spreading out its roots in the deepest places of your heart, acknowledge to yourself whether you would have to die if it were denied you to write. This above all—ask yourself in the stillest hour of your night: *must* I write? Delve into yourself for a deep answer. And if this should be affirmative, if you may meet this earnest question with a strong and simple "*I must*," then build your life according to this necessity.[20]

Knowing the self comes only as we respectfully listen to our inner voices, including our inner necessity. Respectfully means to listen attentively, courteously, and considerately. Most often mixed with the chorus of inner voices is one we could label the critic, the voice that dominates and interrupts the others with judgment or condemnation. Containing the critic in the interests of other still small voices, which have too little air time, is part of the discipline of listening respectfully. Theologian Henri Nouwen states the need well: "It seems that the emphasis on interpersonal sensitivity has at times made us forget to develop the sensitivity that helps us to listen to our own inner voices."[21]

Listening respectfully and sensitively to such questions as What do I know about what I like? What do I value? What do I feel? is an act of self-love. It requires commitment and patience. It takes time and energy "to discover my desires, my rhythms, my tastes, my gifts, my hopes, my wounds."[22]

Also, such listening requires solitude. Solitude carries with it an image of seclusion and isolation, of monks and hermits. Indeed, the word is derived from the Latin *solus*, meaning alone. But solitude is more than being alone. According to Sam Keen, "Solitude begins when a man silences the competing voices of the market, the polis, the home, the mass, and listens to the dictates of his own heart."[23] This solitude of heart is not dependent on being physically separated. It can be "maintained and developed in the center of a big city, in the middle of a large crowd and in the context of a very active and productive life."[24] But practicing solitude can mean withdrawing from familiar roles and a familiar environment, from the routine responsibilities and customary demands of everyday living. For some, sanctuary can be found in the wilderness or at a retreat center; for others, it may take the form of a room apart where quiet refuge can be made. Sam Keen tells of building himself a small cabin as a place of personal sanctuary. To this cabin he brought "icons and sacred objects," childhood items that carried special meaning from his past, and other cherished objects that were part of his life story. He would retreat to this shelter once or twice a week to enjoy solitude, to listen respectfully to his inner self.[25]

For the last twenty years or so, my family and I have vacationed at a small lake in southern Ontario, Canada. By standards of modern convenience, the isolated cabin is crude. (The bath, for instance, is provided by the lake water, which is cool even in August.) In this simple setting, however, we connect with a basic way of life and find sanctuary from the competing voices of our lives. It is this place that has taught me that sometimes we need external support, even a change of environment, in order to create an internal sanctuary of the heart. This retreat has become a place for solitude, a time for discovering myself, a self that often gets lost behind the persona of the caregiver and sometimes caretaker.

Recollecting Our Experience

By respectfully listening to our inner voices we recollect our experiences, because as we listen we inevitably encounter images of our past. The story of our lives is framed within the selected memories of our past experience. Our memories can be hurtful or joyful; they can bring tears to our eyes or smiles to our faces. But they define for us who we are and who are the significant people in our lives. Sam Keen and others emphasize the need and value in "telling our story," recollecting our experience, in the presence of another or others. It is in telling our story that we often discover that our lives are an extension of the wishes, unfulfilled ambitions, and beliefs of others.

Sarah, a thirty-one-year-old architect, made such a discovery after coming to counseling for depression. Her life gave no external indication of her inner pain. Sarah had graduated third in her class at a prestigious university, and had received a major award in her field of study. While many of her classmates were struggling to find employment, Sarah received a lucrative offer to work with a well-established architectural firm. She met and married her husband, Eugene, about two years after she graduated. Their relationship is very fulfilling for both of them. Sarah's present circumstances are not the source of her unhappiness.

But as Sarah recollects her past, it becomes apparent that she decided long ago to make her father, Ronald, proud of her. Shortly after the death of her mother, when Sarah was eleven, Ronald became intently focused on Sarah's academic and athletic achievements. He would attend her field hockey games, often leaving his office early in the day to travel to away games. He frequently consulted with Sarah's teachers about her school courses, sometimes to Sarah's embarrassment. He would also often discuss with Sarah her career choices, but he particularly encouraged her interest in architecture, a profession he would have pursued if he had completed college. (As it was, Ronald had been forced to drop out of college in his second year because of a shortage of finances. He was fortunate to find a job with a drafting firm as an apprentice. Being an ambitious worker, Ronald advanced his career by attending evening courses at a local vocational school and by working long hours.) Through the years, however, Ronald had become quite successful and was now a vice president for the firm he began with as an apprentice. Sarah cares deeply for her father and defends his interest in her accomplishments by saying it shows just how much he cares for her. Through therapy, however, Sarah has seen that she really knows little about what she wants or even how to identify what she wants. As years passed, Sarah became so invested in living out her father's wishes and ambitions that she had lost the ability to decide things for herself, to make choices regarding her life.

Writer and psychologist Harriet Goldhor Lerner identifies this process, that of going along with someone else's agenda for one's life while ignoring one's own wants and insights, as "de-selfing."[26] Despite her achievements, Sarah had lost the connection with her inner self. Her depression and unhappiness were symptoms of her grieving over the loss of self.

By recollecting our experiences we may reclaim the ability to define who we are and who we want to be. As we tell our story in the presence of others, we often distance ourselves from our life experiences. Distancing helps us to see, perhaps for the first time, the unrecognized possibilities of our lives. We identify the wants, hopes, and dreams that we have ignored. Sarah, for example, began to get in touch with a very different part of herself, a more rebellious and opinionated side. She gradually reviewed her life story and reexamined decisions she had made to please her father. She began to ask the questions "What do I believe?" and "What do I want?" and was amazed at how difficult it was for her to identify and to state her own ideas. Eventually she reconsidered her career choice. Although Sarah remains in the field of architecture, she has decided to work with another firm where she will have the opportunity to pursue a more independent approach to her craft. Sarah's insight and new career decision came with difficulty, fear, and trembling. But she began to experience a self behind her persona of compliance.

Cherishing Paradox

When we look within, we discover not one self, but many selves. Thomas Kelly, author of *A Testament of Devotion*, has observed, "Each of us tends to be, not a single self, but a whole committee of selves. There is the civic self, the parental self, the financial self, the literary self. And each of our selves is in turn a rank individualist, not cooperative, but shouting out his voice loudly for himself when the voting time comes."[27] When we observe our multitude of selves, we are confronted with the paradoxical nature of our inner life. Self-intimacy presents us with the need, in Sam Keen's words, to "cherish paradox."

The term *paradox* is defined by such words as contradictory, inconsistent, and ambiguous. But Tournier's phrase "impenetrable mystery" seems to convey the essence of what we encounter in the paradox of the inward journey. No psychological theory or philosophy of human nature can exhaust the mystery of being human. The mysterious is what remains after analysis and explanation have been expended and we are left in silence before that which does not fit our categories, definitions, or common understanding. Cherishing paradox means we are always surprised by what we discover within, and that we value ourselves in the process of becoming. And we come to appreciate the dynamic and sometimes opposing forces that make up our inner life.

Some people are so frightened by the paradox they find within themselves that they embrace and adhere to a particular self-definition or social role and resist any new or contradictory insight or information. Aaron, for example, a forty-five-year-old computer programmer, described himself as an aggressive and pragmatic thinker. He approached most of the issues of his life with a stance of detached logic. He often compared himself with pride to the character of Mr. Spock from the television series *Star Trek*. He refused the suggestion of some of his friends that he was a person of deep feeling. During counseling sessions it was proposed to Aaron that perhaps he had adopted his detached and logical self-image in response to his rigid upbringing. He responded defensively, even denying that his family background had anything to do with the kind of person he was today. For Aaron, the thought that there may be a gentle, tender part of himself was as alien as the idea that he had antennae.

At the other extreme, there are people whose boundaries are so fluid that they can shift from self to self as their environment and relationships change. These people lack a center core of self-definition. It is the particular setting that defines who they will be in any given moment. The character of Leonard Zelig in the Woody Allen film *Zelig* provides a classic portrayal of the person who shifts selves with whomever he meets. When in Rome, Zelig not only does as the Romans do, he becomes a Roman. He is so good at merging with others that he loses all contact with himself. He forfeits any uniqueness in his personality. Because Zelig is a newsworthy figure his problem is recognized, and he is dubbed by the press as "the chameleon man."

Cherishing our paradox means valuing the diversity within ourselves and staying aware of the variety of selves that live within us. Maintaining an observing self, which keeps us in touch with the constant movement of our feelings, thoughts, beliefs, and needs, will prevent us from identifying with any one self to the exclusion of the others. The ability to maintain this observing self is a necessary ingredient of self-intimacy.

Loving What We Cannot Understand

Self-intimacy also requires that we love within ourselves what we cannot reduce to understanding. Pioneering psychologist C.G. Jung once commented on our tendency to become self-critical in dealing with that in ourselves that we do not understand.

> That I feed the beggar, that I forgive an insult, that I love my enemy in the name of Christ—all these are undoubtedly great virtues. What I do unto the least of my brethren, that I do unto Christ. But what if I should discover that the least amongst them all, the poorest of all beggars, the most impudent of all offenders, yea, the very fiend himself, that these are within me, and that I myself stand in need of the arms of my own kindness, that I myself am the enemy who must be loved. What then? Then, as a rule, the whole truth of Christianity is reversed. Then there is no more talk of love and long-suffering. We say to the brother with us, 'Raca' [a term of reproach or insult, indicating a person who is contemptible in some way[28]], and condemn and rage against ourselves. We hide him from the world, we deny ever having met this least among the lowly in ourselves.[29]

We return then to where we began, the need for healthy self-love. Self-love does not depend on our ability to understand all that is going on within ourselves. Rather, it is promoted by an empathetic acceptance of that which we do not understand. It means that we approach ourselves—our shortcomings, idiosyncracies, and limitations—with a nonjudgmental attitude.

It is on this foundation of healthy self-love that we are able to reach out in love to others. Again, the words of Erich Fromm: "Respect for one's own integrity and uniqueness, love for and understanding of one's ownself, cannot be separated from respect and love and understanding for another individual. The love for my own self is inseparably connected with the love for any other being."[30]

Making Connection with Others

Making an intimate connection with another person means a certain resonance of souls, an opening up between people that permits each a glimpse into the inner life of the other. This soul connection is a mysterious occurrence, an event which we cannot reason ourselves into or out of.[31] Such a connection of souls is Martin Buber's "I-Thou" encounter, as distinguished from an "I-it" encounter; it is a meeting of persons that cannot be produced or planned, only received as a gift. Yet when this blessed event occurs, it becomes the basis for our commitment and devotion to the life and growth of the other. Once such an intimate connection is made, we experience a bond that even time and circumstance cannot disrupt. In the words of philosopher Gabriel Marcel: "Even if I cannot see you, if I cannot touch you, I feel that you are with me."[32]

When this inner connection between people occurs, we experience another's wholeness. The word *wholeness* here is intended to convey a particular perspective in which we do not fragment the other person into this or that characteristic, but intuitively experience the other as a unique individual apart from ourselves.

The words of Thomas and Patrick Malone at the beginning of the chapter, "When you can be in your own personal space while you are also in the space you share with another, you are being intimate," provide an excellent description of the hidden movements of intimacy. Being in one's own space describes the movement from dependence to independence. Dependence is our first state of being, the stage of development in which our survival depends upon our ability to lure others into meeting our basic needs for food, protection, and nurture. For a significant portion of our lives we rely on the nurturing instincts of others. But the time comes for us to define our own space, to risk resisting the unwritten demands to conform and adjust to expectations of others. At first, the movement toward independence may take the form of "positive rebellion" against rules and values we believe are being imposed upon us.[33]

Some rebellion is not, however, a move toward independence, but rather a covert effort to make others feel guilty and responsible for our lives. Beneath these gestures of independence is an assumption of entitlement that demands that others meet our needs and expectations. Rebellion in this case is not the same as autonomy. Creating our own space, our own identity, requires not only breaking from established rules and authority; it is a willingness to be responsible for our own life, for our own choices.

The journey to becoming an individual can be rough indeed. In many cultures, there are rites of passage into adulthood which require a young person to break from dependency, to perform deeds of courage and self-sufficiency that demonstrate independence. But in contemporary Western culture such passages are often more private and peculiar to each individual. Lynn's story is not uncommon. Following college, Lynn had returned to her parents' home while she looked for a teaching job. Although Lynn and her parents, Dale and Josephine, had many conversations in preparation for her return home and had agreed on some sharing of responsibilities, the transition proved much more difficult than either Lynn or her parents had anticipated. Lynn resented her parents asking, for example, when she would be returning home in the evening.

"It's as though I am still in grade school," Lynn complains. Her parents, on the other hand, are distressed at Lynn's apparent lack of concern for their worry about her being late.

"Why can't you see that we aren't checking up on you?" Josephine says to Lynn during one exasperating interchange. "Are we supposed to stop caring because you have gone away to college?"

At times, Dale and Josephine also are at odds regarding how to respond to Lynn's behavior. Dale begins to distance himself from the situation, especially during shouting episodes between Lynn and her mother, and he is critical of his wife for not backing off from these confrontations. Josephine begins to feel deserted by Dale and resents being the focus of Lynn's attacks. Clearly, Lynn's return home precipitated a struggle of dependency and independence.

When Lynn discussed the situation with members of her support group, she gained a significant understanding of her role in this struggle. After listening to Lynn's complaints about her parents, one member of the group asked Lynn what she thought she was doing to keep the struggle going. The question was familiar because group members had long before committed themselves to holding each other accountable. Lynn was strained to respond. Eventually, she acknowledged that by returning home to live she assumed that her parents would rescue her from her present difficulties; that although she was claiming independence, she was clinging to her identity as her parents' child. And, perhaps more significant, Lynn recognized that interpreting her parents' comments as interferences, rather than as statements of concern, only encouraged their anxiety and questioning. In fact, both Lynn and her parents were in the throes of redefining their relationship and needed the patience and understanding of each other in this process.

Lynn's experience in her support group provided her with an opportunity to move a step further through her passage into independence. Discussing her dilemma and receiving the response of other members of the group opened Lynn's consciousness to her holding on to dependency, and the group's encouragement gave Lynn the support she needed to take responsibility for her own choices and situation.

If independence involves establishing one's own space, interdependence is, paraphrasing the words of the Malones, being in one's own personal space while also being in the space shared with another. Interdependence accommodates the appropriate dependency needs of each partner while also granting each room for independent thought, feelings, and actions. Interdependence assumes that each person has clear boundaries of physical and emotional space, yet these are permeable, open enough to permit each to share the thoughts and feelings of the other.

The biblical concept of hospitality is a fitting image of the interconnectedness that intimacy brings. Writer Henri Nouwen reminds us that many biblical stories show the importance of welcoming strangers into our homes, and that such strangers often carry precious gifts for the amiable host.[34] Emotionally and spiritually, being a receptive host means being at home in ourselves and thereby available to the guest, whether a spouse, child, colleague, friend, or stranger. It requires that we not be so filled with our own needs, opinions, and advice that we have no room to attentively listen to the views and feelings of others.

Being receptive and even listening attentively may, however, be only a part of what we need in relating intimately to others. Frequently, we must show active concern. But as we act in support of another, it is important to clarify the distinction between rescuing and caring. Rescuing is motivated by our need to be needed rather than by the needs of the other. Often the need of the other is only an occasion for maintaining our identity as good helpers. (This is the caretaker role we discussed in chapter 3.) Our own need to rescue is often met by the resistance of those we are trying to "help" and by our feelings of being unappreciated and fatigued. Rescuing is a quiet dominance; it lacks mutuality and cooperation. When the expected outcome is not forthcoming, the rescuer's need for dominance is often exposed by his or her switch from rescuing to persecuting.

Caring is more concerned for the dignity and integrity of the person being helped than for the particular problem or need. It emphasizes mutual respect and cooperative effort. It does not forget who owns the problem. Because caring is not filled with the need to be helpful, it makes room for the other person to struggle with the problem and to explore his or her own potential. Caring can tolerate promise without certainty of outcome; it can examine possibilities without being invested in one in particular. Caring creates space for the other to grow, to doubt, to question, and to dream; and it brings a firm belief in the other's ability to think clearly, to feel deeply, and to act decisively on their own behalf. Caring affirms another's capability in defining his wants or envisioning her possibilities.

Making Connection with Creation

The polarity of dominance and cooperation prevalent in human relating is particularly relevant also in our connecting with the created order. Increasingly, we are being reminded of the interactive nature of all creation. As we move from a model of nature that is based on the assumption of human dominance, we begin to see that intimacy is not confined to human relationships but includes the connection with all life. Author Marilyn Ferguson writes that new scientific knowledge "reveals a rich, creative, dynamic, interconnected reality. Nature, we are learning, is not a force over which we must triumph but the medium of our transformation."[35] Science, it seems, is confirming what poets, philosophers, and diverse disciplines and traditions have been affirming for centuries: nature has an interconnected quality. Researchers of ancient religions and native American spirituality; ecological pioneers like John Seed, who speaks of a "Council of All Beings"; and modern scientists such as Brian Swimme, author of *The Universe Is a Green Dragon*, are redefining for us the transitory qualities of the universe. All agree on the fundamental truth that we are intimately connected with the created order, that we are transformed by our interaction with all life.

Writers such as Annie Dillard and anthropologist Loren Eiseley give us a new appreciation for the immense voices that speak to us through the cycles and dynamics of the natural world. They have modeled for us a new way of listening and learning from the parables of the universe. The "I-Thou" relationship is not confined to human interaction; it is a mode of being that we can experience in all our encounters with the natural order. Approaching the natural world as though to a "Thou" involves honoring and appreciating the created order as a part of the great chain of being that includes us all. In the words of St. John of the Cross: his beloved is "the mountains, the solitary wooded valleys, strange islands . . . silent music."[36]

Jesus' use of metaphors of nature—the lilies of the field, birds of the air, the mustard seed—as illustrations for understanding the workings of the reign of God implies a connection between the cycles of nature and the Spirit at work in human life. When Jesus invites us to consider the lilies of the field, for example, he is reminding us to simply be. The lilies do not toil or spin. Their growth is not the result of anxious effort but is rather the consequence of the natural course of their being. For Jesus, nature resounded with the silent music that gives witness to the Creator. Undergirding the lilies, the birds, and all life is the sustaining love of One who relates to us at the very core of our inner being.

Making Connection with the Divine Other

Theologian William Johnston has observed that "in the journey into the dark being of another, one may get fleeting glimpses of that other's personal core. These glimpses are momentary and passing; they are cosmic experiences of God, because God is the center of the other's being."[37] Each "I-Thou" encounter, each glimmer into the inner self of another, opens the aperture of our hearts to see and to experience the Eternal. Yet even as we glance through to the eternal Thou, we discover that the eternal Thou is reaching out to us. Although we see only dimly and understand only in part, we are seen clearly and are fully understood by One who loves and accepts us.

The ultimate expression of spirituality is for us to experience an intimate relationship with the Divine, to confront and to be transformed by the eternal Thou. A primal portrayal of divine-human intimacy is presented in the Book of Job. The relationship between Job and God is a relationship between an I and a Thou. In the words of philosopher William Barrett, the encounter between Job and God is on the "level of existence" not simply the level of reason; it is a "confrontation of the whole man, Job, in the fullness and violence of his passion with the unknowable and overwhelming God."[38] Barrett reminds us that Job's relationship with God is one of faith: "this faith takes on varying shapes of revolt, anger, dismay, and confusion. Job says, *'Though he slay me, yet will I trust in him,'* but he adds . . . *'But I will maintain my own ways before him.'* Job retains his own identity ('his own ways') in confronting the Creator before whom he is as Nothing."[39] Job not only maintains his "I-ness" before the Almighty, but expresses his anger as well.

Faith in the context of intimate relationships is not an intellectual assent to articles of belief or to a creed; "faith is trust before it is belief."[40] Faith in the deepest sense is an opening of one's thoughts and feelings, one's inner being to another. Faith in relating to others means taking the risks of being honest and vulnerable. It has been suggested that just as sexual pleasure is enhanced by giving up control and learning to surrender to a natural body function, so having the faith to surrender to our most vulnerable and honest feelings is the route to making loving contact with others.[41]

According to Barrett, "faith is the openness of the whole man toward his God, and therefore must be able to encompass all human modes of being."[42] At the risk of oversimplifying, it may be said that religion is talking about God; spirituality is relating to God. Religion is the outward expression of faith; spirituality is faith expressed through the inward opening of ourselves to the transforming power of God's love.

The story of Job reminds us again of the importance of having a sense of "I" while being open and in communion with another, even when the other is the Other. As the confrontation between God and Job unfolds, God also becomes angry and confronts Job with the mysteries of the universe. Job finally recognizes that although he knew God from the Hebrew teachings, he now knows God from the experience of the struggle to communicate his perspective and pain: "I had heard of you by the hearing of the ear, but now my eye sees you."[43]

In addressing the issue of communion and autonomy, writer and theologian William Johnston introduces the distinction between merging and indwelling. Merging is an unfree attachment, a coming together in which individual identity is lost; there is progressive diminishment of the distinction between the "I" and the "Thou." Indwelling, by contrast, is a mutuality of love and trust, freed from attachment, in which we are not absorbed into one another nor do we lose our personal and distinct identity.[44]

When Jesus says to his disciples: "Abide in me as I abide in you"[45] or Paul speaks of being "in Christ" as Christ is in him, they are describing the experience of indwelling, a coming together in love and trust in which the autonomous personalities are not reduced, but expanded to deeper, authentic selves.[46]

In one way or another, we are changed through our relationships. We are amused when we notice couples or friends who have been together for a number of years taking on common features. There is often a subtle merging, for example, of personality traits, of personal tastes or values, or even of physical appearance. In relating to God or to each other in an intimate relationship, we are not merged into nonidentity; rather, our personal sense of "I" is expanded through our relationship with the Eternal, progressively and lovingly transformed by One who accepts and calls forth even our hidden, disowned selves.[47]

Chapter Six

Building Communities of Personal Support

There are thousands of local churches in the United States, representing an enormous range of variation in doctrine and worship. Yet most define themselves as communities of personal support.

From Habits of the Heart

The closer we come to the heart of the One who loves us with an unconditional love, the closer we come to each other in the solidarity of a redeemed humanity.

Henri J. M. Nouwen

Church as Intimate Community

The image of home, author and theologian Henri Nouwen says, carries the qualities of intimacy, a place that offers the sense of belonging. With that sense of belonging come other evocative qualities of hearth, the sense of warmth and protection, the feeling of care and love. Saying, "I do not feel at home here," expresses an experience of not belonging; to say, "I wish I were home," declares our desire to be welcomed with open arms.[1]

Jesus' story of the prodigal son is a paradigm of "coming home." We picture the jubilant father embracing his exhausted son, who has squandered his fortune in his travels and has now returned home. The story suggests our universal yearning for acceptance and expresses our longing to find intimacy at all levels of our lives.

The research of Robert Bellah and his colleagues journaled in their book *Habits of the Heart* suggests that many people who participate in local congregations are seeking a personal, intimate community that has the characteristics of home—warmth, caring, and acceptance.[2] Yet many who are drawn to the church in their quest for community are severely disappointed and may redirect their pursuit to other forms of personal growth, other support groups that have proliferated during the last several years.

The latter half of the twentieth century has seen large numbers of people struggling with and yearning for contact with the sacred. The doubting 1960s question "Is God dead?" and the criticism of hypocrisy within the church have shifted in the 1990s. Many adults, in having grown to maturity and parenthood themselves, are taking a second look at religion and spirituality, seeking meaning and spiritual direction in their lives.[3] Organized religion has attempted to accommodate this yearning by coaxing Americans back into places of worship.

In the Middle Ages, before the schisms shattered Catholicism into so many ideological splinters, the community was the church, for good or ill. As mythologist and scholar Joseph Campbell points out, the church was the largest physical structure in the village and not only dominated the landscape but also the lives of the people.

Since that time, churches have gradually ceased to be the center of Western culture. Campbell notes that the tallest buildings in today's world are the financial institutions; witness the giant twin towers that comprise the World Trade Center in New York City.

Yet there remains a deep yearning for personal communities of support; the search for intimacy will not be denied. But there is much that is competing today with the institution of the church. People seeking answers to their questions of intimacy in therapy rooms, in self-help books, or within sundry groups may find either healthy expression in communities that encourage diversity, inclusiveness, and solidarity or in groups that promote conformity, exclusivity, and fear. Few might expect the church to provide direction on this fundamental human quest for intimacy.

Genuine intimacy relies partly on a balancing of the two primary urges of autonomy and communion. And as we have seen, these two urges (the quest for individuality and the yearning for togetherness) may be distorted into fearful distance and fearful closeness. Fearful autonomy can also be expressed as the tendency to assert dominance and control over others and over the created order; fearful communion as the tendency to surrender the self, to seek union with a greater whole, even to the point of giving up responsibility for one's own decisions and life.

These tendencies are not only expressed by individuals in the context of dyadic relationships, they are also apparent in group settings, whether of a club, a congregation, or a family. The power of a group to influence our thinking and behavior is enormous. The relatively new field of family theory, for example, has helped us to see how the behavior and feelings of an individual family member are often a reflection of hidden, frequently unconscious dynamics within the family as a whole.[4] When we understand the subtle nature of group dynamics, we can appreciate the interconnected nature of life. In the words of philosopher Martin Buber: "All real living is meeting."[5]

The fearful distance and fearful closeness that permeate our relationships with one another as individuals also affect our life together in groups. Groups based on fear tend to be exclusive; they find ways to distance themselves from others and discriminate against those who do not fit their pattern of group membership. Such group emphasis on differences is not balanced by an appreciation of the unique gifts and contributions of other people. It is used rather as a way of maintaining an elitist attitude in relating to the outside world. Exclusive groups foster fearful closeness by requiring conformity of style, values, language, and even appearance on the part of those who are on the inside. They can become cliques and cults of conformity that often have an air of moral superiority: "God, I thank you that I am not like other people"[6] says a character in one of Jesus' stories.

The closeness that such exclusive groups promise and promote can be tremendously attractive to people who lack a sense of self-definition, who are looking for an identity to adopt. They appeal to those who feel isolated and alone and want desperately to belong to something.

Bruce was such a person. Raised in a conservative religious home, he was active in his church's youth group throughout his junior and senior high school years. In many ways life was easy for Bruce during those years. He did exceptionally well academically, played actively in intramural sports, and displayed an unusual talent as a musician. People who knew Bruce expected him to be a success in whatever he pursued. Yet Bruce had many acquaintances but few friends. There was an emptiness inside of him that surfaced after he began college.

Reflecting on his experience later, Bruce commented that while in high school his life was structured by others and he adapted well to the expectations they had of him, whether teachers, parents, or other authority figures. But when he began college, Bruce was suddenly faced with the task of making new friends and reestablishing himself among people who did not know him. The task became overwhelming. Perhaps for the first time in his life, Bruce experienced real loneliness. He attended a small Christian gathering on campus, hoping to make new friends, but he soon dropped out because, in his words, "They acted like children."

It was in the second semester of his sophomore year that Bruce met Greg, a part-time student at the same university. While Bruce was reserved, Greg was brash and even at times defiant; while Bruce was serious and determined, Greg was playful and seldom exerted himself academically. In many ways Greg represented all that Bruce had avoided being. However, the two young men became quick friends.

It was at a party at Greg's apartment that Bruce met Lyle and Skip, two of Greg's close friends from high school. The four formed an immediate and strong attachment, on weekends spending a great deal of time together drinking, watching sports events on television, and conversing, as Bruce later described it. The group was for Bruce a haven from the loneliness he had experienced. With these three young men he felt accepted and respected. Bruce spoke more openly with Greg, Lyle, and Skip than he had ever done with anybody else. The group had become for him a second family, a fact which did not go unnoticed by his parents. They expressed concern at the amount of time Bruce spent with his new friends and the lack of contact with themselves.

A turning point in Bruce's relationship to the group occurred, however, when Marcie became a part of his life. Marcie and Bruce met in a class at the university. Bruce had never been in love before, but Marcie captured his heart. As the two increasingly spent more time together, Bruce became less available for regular gatherings with Greg, Lyle, and Skip. At first, the other men poked fun at Bruce's "new love," but beneath the humor there was a hint of rejection. As time passed, the tensions became more exposed and expressed, even to the point of open conflict between Greg and Bruce. In his confusion and dismay by the opposition of his friends to his new relationship, Bruce discovered a hidden rule of membership in the group: "Thou shalt have no other loyalties before us."

After a conversation with the campus chaplain, Bruce decided to discuss the situation openly with the three young men, particularly his feeling of disappointment and his need for their acceptance of his relationship with Marcie. Bruce genuinely desired to preserve his friendship with the group, and in a nonaccusing manner he tried to raise the topic with them. But they remained obdurate; they persisted in interpreting his relationship with Marcie as a rebuke of the group. Bruce soon realized that commitment for this group meant inflexible loyalty and availability to the group's ends. The members were not committed to the personal growth and well-being of individual members. Bruce's acceptance by the men had come with the price tag of loss of personal feelings and needs, a price Bruce was not unwilling to pay. As Bruce reflected on his experience, he wondered whether he would have had the courage to leg go of his attachment to the group if Marcie had not been there to support him. Perhaps, Bruce mused, his relationship with Marcie was his way of acknowledging what his conscious mind could not admit, that his relationship with the group had become destructive to his deepest self. He felt chagrined at how subtly he had been willing to forfeit his personal freedom for the security and acceptance of the group.

The experience of Bruce seems mild when compared to the destructiveness that exclusive groups have inflicted on others in our world. We need only to think of groups such as the Ku Klux Klan to realize the damaging potential of exclusivity. Such cliques or organizations create a pseudointimacy. They promise security, identity, acceptance, and a sense of purpose that temporarily overcome personal insecurities and inadequacies and provide a sense of belonging. But they also encourage their members to see those on the outside not only as wrong but also as dangerous. The fearful distancing by such groups requires an enemy, who is portrayed as malevolent and upon whom the group inflicts all forms of criticism and hostility. Exclusive groups are characterized by oppositional thinking: They know more about what they are against than what they are for.

Exclusivity is not limited to extremist groups, however. It is a mind-set that can penetrate the most charitable and sincere groups. Whenever a group or organization, liberal or conservative, religious or secular, begins to define itself in opposition to others, or fails to appreciate the value of diverse points of view, then it is in danger of becoming elitist. Also, exclusive groups cannot impart intimacy because they promote the very conditions that prevent intimate relationships.

"True communities," according to psychiatrist M. Scott Peck, "are always reaching to extend themselves. . . . There is an 'allness' to community."[7] Genuine community is inclusive and celebrates diversity; it honors the variety of gifts of its members. Real community includes not only people with differences but also the differences within each person.

Celebrating diversity does not, however, mean that real community is being all things to all people. A group with no common sense of identity is like an individual with no sense of "I-ness." It is crucial for a group to define and affirm its distinctiveness. Yet designating a group's particular qualities needs to be balanced by an appreciation of the diversity of its members' differing perceptions, opinions, and gifts. It is in respecting this variety of differences that a group keeps from degenerating into an exclusive club or clique, and makes intimacy possible.

The church, at its best, fosters community by encouraging self-identity (by nurturing Christian growth) and also diversity (by welcoming strangers). How should the church foster community? The paradox is that we believe it can do so not so much by focusing on community as a major goal but by creating mature Christians. People who grow in their love of Christ and in service to the world about which God cares so deeply form into a natural community. After a time spent in worship, service, and personal healing and growth, people dimly sense they are living members of Christ's body.

Communion as a Symbol of Intimacy

When we invite others into our home, whether luxurious or humble, we share what we have of ourselves. The key word here is share—whether a sheltering roof from the storm, a glass of refreshing water, or a simple meal. The often-neglected custom of saying grace before meals reminds us that sharing a meal was once an important intimate event. The recitation of grace lends itself not only to a sense of spiritual centering on the inside but also to a sense of community on the outside. With grace, every meal becomes a ritual, every day becomes a thanksgiving.

So sharing implies a sense of mutuality, a sense of communion with another. We do not give away what it is that we have; we divide it and enjoy it together. So it is with the sacrament of communion, an occasion of communing—or sharing—with others.

Rabbi Harold Kushner has observed that "because of the emotional and biological importance of food, sharing a meal used to be considered a significantly intimate event. . . . It was a way of making the participants feel that they were linked to each other by the shared meal. Christians will recognize the significance of communion, a symbolic shared meal derived from the Last Supper which Jesus shared with his disciples, as a way of linking them not only to God but to their fellow communicants. (Note the relationship between the words communion and community.)"[8]

Mythologist and scholar Joseph Campbell regards communion as a deeply spiritual act. Reflecting with journalist Bill Moyers in "The Power of Myth" about his own past experience as a practicing Roman Catholic, he says:

> One of the wonderful things in the Catholic ritual is going to communion. There you are taught that this *is* the body and blood of the Savior. And you take it into you, and you turn inward, and there Christ is the spirit in you. You see people coming back from communion, and they are inward-turned, they really are.[9]

Most Protestant denominations concentrate on the entire act of the communion service rather than primarily on the elements of bread and wine. The act of distributing these elements, of reenacting the ritual of breaking the bread and pouring the wine and sharing in the sacrament together, is a remembering that we are bound together in the Spirit that is within and between us. Communion is then an experience of indwelling. We are one with the Spirit, yet retain our unique identity; and we are one with others in the community while celebrating our diversity. Communion is more than an act of personal spiritual renewal. It is also a reestablishment of our identity as a community of faith. Communion leads us, it is hoped, to a deeper sense of community.

Closely connected with communion as an expression of intimacy is the experience of prayer. Although the church has traditionally emphasized the place of intercessory prayer (prayer on behalf of others) as a part of spiritual discipline, prayer typically becomes a private matter, focusing on oneself or those who are close. Some have relegated prayer to primarily a psychological function that affects the attitude of the person praying. Yet many people who sincerely and regularly intercede for others perceive such prayer as a means of bringing about a particular change, either of circumstance or attitude. Physician Larry Dossey in his provocative book *Recovering the Soul: A Scientific and Spiritual Search* takes issue with those who advocate prayer for specific outcomes. He refers to a number of studies on the effectiveness of prayer in healing that suggest "nondirected prayer moves organisms toward those states of form and function that are best for them, and that the practitioner need not know what 'best' is."[10] Underlying this conclusion is the clear indication that prayer is our connecting link with the Universal Mind, the spiritual reality that unites us with all life. Such studies serve to undergird what sages and the faithful of all ages have known: Prayer is not restricted to the confines of an individual, nor is it intended to influence the mind of the Almighty; rather, prayer is an expression of the life connection that permeates the whole of the universe. It is the "primal speech"[11] that connects us with the One who seeks our best. Prayer so understood is the ultimate expression of intimacy, a reflection of the intimate reality of the universe.

Although we have been placing emphasis on intimacy in the context of human-to-human relationships, it is important to stress again that intimacy has to do with making life connections in whatever form and context that may occur. "Connection," according to psychiatrists Thomas and Patrick Malone, "is simply our personal participation in truth."[12] Such times of connection, whether they come in relating to the stars or the sky, to the Earth, or to your neighbor, are a reminder of our participation in the truth of the universe and our relationship to all life. It is out of such sacramental moments that we realize that intimacy is not restricted to one dimension of life, but rather is our interconnectedness with all life.

Building Personal Support

It is out of our deep interconnectedness with all life, out of our recognition of our common participation in truth, that community is born. But community, like intimacy itself, is often misunderstood. The word *community* has become distorted; it often refers to towns, churches, clubs, or professional organizations. Community is hardly an appropriate word for those who are a part of such groups and organizations that may communicate little or not at all with each other and know little or nothing about each other's lives.[13] M. Scott Peck reminds us: "Our hometowns may well be geographical collections of human beings with tax and political structures in common, but precious little else relates them to each other. Towns are not, in any meaningful sense of the word, communities."[14] Churches also are often gatherings of people who perhaps share a tradition, some common values and commitments, but few could be described as intimate communities. There is also a danger of idealizing the idea of community. Just as there are no perfect couples or families, there also are no perfect communities. Building community is a process, and when it comes, it is a gift.

Community is not easy to portray to one who has not known it, and most people have not had an experience of community. Yet it is important to describe some of the elements of true community, although like intimacy in general, no description can exhaust the experience or do justice to it. We have already emphasized that true community is inclusive, always seeking to expand itself, to extend its boundaries to include the unfamiliar. In the words of Peck: "It is not merely a matter of including different sexes, races, and creeds. It is also inclusive of the full range of human emotions. Tears are as welcome as laughter, fear as well as faith."[15] But if true community aspires to extend its boundaries, it also endeavors to respect the boundaries of self and others.

Language is a primary way we respect boundaries, in which we include or exclude ourselves and others. Through our choice of words, for example, we include or exclude the cause of our emotions. When we say "You make me angry!" we exclude the angry feelings as a part of ourselves and project them: they are caused by "you," someone outside of ourselves. Being responsible for and owning our own feelings, perspectives, needs, and behaviors is an expression of inclusion. No true community can grow as long as its members hold others responsible for their emotional responses or behavior.

Another familiar and common way we see the power of language to exclude is through the use of sexist, racist, and ageist vocabulary. We frequently assume that people in positions of power, responsibility, and authority are *he*, while inanimate objects, such as battleships and automobiles, are referred to as *she*. Many people have viewed the use of inclusive language—even as simple a change as chairman to chair or chairperson, for instance—as intrusive, ridiculous, or inconvenient. But exploring alternatives and making changes in language are ways to remind ourselves of our circuitous tendency to discriminate and exclude. Philosopher Martin Buber's description of "I-Thou" and "I-It" relationships can help in clarifying the subtleties in the use of language to fragment. When we refer to others in ways that tend to depersonalize, to treat them as *its* rather than *thous*, we are violating their integrity and destroying the possibility of community.

But if language can be an instrument of discrimination and exclusion, it can also be a means for building bridges between the worlds of people, for creating mutual understanding, for conveying respect and care, and for providing a sense of safety, all of which are necessary for developing trust and community. In the words of therapists John Amodeo and Kris Wentworth: "The use of language is the primary vehicle through which we share our inner world of feelings, meanings, values, and thoughts with others."[16] And learning to speak our truth—our deepest feelings and meanings—to others, while at the same time respecting the right of others to respond from their own felt experience, their own truth, can do much to build the trust and openness from which real community grows.[17]

Perhaps one of the most difficult skills to develop is that of communicating our feelings, meanings, and needs without resorting to blame, criticism, attack, or moralizing as means to get others to change or to give us what we want. Communication that holds others responsible for how we feel or behave, or communication that is focused to change another, can only hinder the progress toward community. When we are on the receiving end of these judgments, criticisms, and blame, we realize how quickly we can shut down or withdraw. Yet we normally receive little help in learning to speak our experience in a simple, direct, and noncoercive manner.[18]

Therapists Amodeo and Wentworth have suggested a three-step process for communicating in a self-revealing and noncoercive way.[19] This process constitutes a way of tangibly establishing respectful boundaries between self and others.

First, we need to identify the specific action or behavior that upsets or dissatisfies us and noncritically express our feelings to the other person. This step encourages us to describe our own feelings rather than focus on the other person's behavior. When we assume to know or when we judge the other's motives or intentions, we may solicit a defensive response. Statements such as "You don't care about our relationship or you would want to spend more time with me!" make the assumption that the other person doesn't care, and it may understandably meet with resistance. We are much more likely to be heard if we state our concern in a way in which we take responsibility for our own feelings: "When we don't spend time together, I feel uncared for in our relationship."

Second, we need to express our resulting feelings and thoughts as simply, accurately, and concisely as possible. This step helps us connect with our felt experience. Often, as we stated earlier, our initial feeling responses may cover deeper, more primal feelings that are overlooked if we act too quickly and without reflection. Anger, for example, can often hide feelings of sadness or fear.

Third, we need to request what we want or need from the other person in order to feel more nourished and loved. We are often raised to ignore what we want. Sometimes it is a more familiar response to be angry, or to feel rejected or unloved than to be clear about our underlying needs or wants. Our feelings often indicate unmet needs. But stating our needs may not always get us what we want, as the other person also has the right to choose not to give us what we request. However, clear requests are more likely to be honored, even during those times when the other person does not respond as we would like, affirm our needs, and validate or respect our inner self.

Even genuine communities have border skirmishes, times when boundaries need to be clarified or redefined. Confrontation and conflict in community do not result, however, in division or in taking sides. Rather, they provide an opportunity for people to expand their perspectives and to confront their differences in a way that does not lead to rejection or factionalism. "A community is a group that can fight gracefully."[20] This is true because undergirding the community is a commitment to persevere within the process of growing trust and understanding.

Yet there are times when disagreement can lead to a decision to separate and to take different paths. Such moments can be extremely painful, regardless of how the separation is initiated. During these periods it is difficult to remain open to our own hurt and to take responsibility for our own part in the separation.[21] Intimacy means that even such experiences can lead us to become clearer about our own deepest needs and respectful of the right of the other person to make choices different from our own.

Perhaps the most difficult message for us to hear is that the quest for true community also leads us beyond helpfulness, that being helpful sometimes is detrimental to community. When we see hurt, we want to heal it; when we meet pain, we want to alleviate it; when we encounter brokenness, we want to fix it. What could be more natural? Or more loving? Yet our inclination to help often arises in response to our own discomfort and feeling of helplessness, not in response to the need of the other. M. Scott Peck states it bluntly: "Almost all . . . attempts to convert and heal are not only naive and ineffective but quite self-centered and self-serving."[22] Perhaps our most difficult struggle is to be in the presence of another's hurt, pain, or brokenness and and to do nothing, thereby experiencing the helplessness and vulnerability.

True community is not built on our efforts to heal or fix others. In fact, nothing can destroy community faster than each person trying to help, advise, or heal another. Such attempts at "helpfulness," no matter how well intended, most often originate in the view that other people are hurts to be healed or problems to be solved—*Its* rather than *Thous*. In the words of Peck: "The fact of the matter is that often the most loving thing we can do when a friend is in pain is to *share* that pain—to be there even when we have nothing to offer except our presence and even when being there is painful to ourselves."[23]

Offering our presence does not necessarily mean being silent, however. We can clarify the situation, encourage the person, explore possibilities with the person, and confront the obstacles. But most of all, we can offer what rabbi and family therapist Edwin Friedman calls "nonanxious presence."[24] Our capacity to recognize and to contain our own anxiousness in the face of life's struggles largely determines our ability to be a healing force in the lives of others. Rabbi Friedman focuses on two aspects of nonanxious presence that are particularly relevant for creating community: "the value of playfulness and the dangers of diagnosis."[25]

Playfulness is the antidote to our tendency to become overly serious or "helpful" in the face of problems. According to Friedman,

> Seriousness is more than an attitude; it is a total orientation, a way of thinking embedded in constant, chronic anxiety. It is characterized by lack of flexibility in response, a narrow repertoire of approaches, persistent efforts to try harder, an inability to change direction, and a loss of perspective and concentrated focus.[26]

Playfulness encourages detached concern, an ability to be flexible in response, and a broadening of our view of our problem. As Friedman reminds us, playfulness does not have to do with one-liners nor with quick come-backs.[27] Nor is playfulness sarcasm, which is often the way anger is expressed, in the guise of humor. Playfulness is a way of breaking out of the cycle of overseriousness while at the same time staying in contact with and appropriately responsible for the problem at hand.

If seriousness is the way we often stay stuck in a cycle of anxiety, diagnosing or labeling of others is frequently the way we deal with our own anxiety. According to Friedman, "A good rule of thumb is that if you catch yourself diagnosing someone else, there is probably something in you that you are trying to hide."[28] Again we are reminded of Jesus' words regarding judging others: "Why do you see the speck in your neighbor's eye, but do not notice the log in your own eye?"[29] Here Jesus combines humor (picture a log in someone's eye!) with confrontation by reminding his listeners that when they focus on others through judgment, diagnosis, or labeling they are avoiding their own anxious concerns. It is perhaps not accidental that Jesus' words pertaining to judgment follow on his comments regarding anxiousness.

Structures for Intimacy

Pastors and church committees seeking to promote genuine intimate connections within their congregations might well take cues from the outsiders meeting down the hall. Those groups are the "anonymous" fellowships (often meeting in church fellowship rooms, YWCA offices, and hospital cafeterias), a multitude of therapy programs based on the twelve steps and twelve traditions of Alcoholics Anonymous. These groups can offer great insights and spiritual guidance to churches seeking to revitalize their flocks and to make churchgoing a meaningful and intimate experience.

Although support groups of all kinds are enjoying a growing popularity, it is the twelve-step movement that emphasizes spirituality as crucial to true support. First, a little information about the roots of the twelve-step movement.

It was more than fifty years ago that two hopeless alcoholics, Dr. Bob S. and Bill W., had their first historic meeting in Akron, Ohio. They developed a structure called Alcoholics Anonymous, which was to offer the miracle of healing to thousands of alcoholics, women and men whose lives were spinning out of control because of alcohol. In the last ten years, the fellowship has experienced its greatest growth. Since 1978 membership in A.A. has shot up from 400,000 to more than one million people. Thousands more have adapted the precepts of A.A. to form groups to aid other drug addicts; adults who were reared in alcoholic, dysfunctional, or abusive families; compulsive overeaters; sexual compulsives; and families and friends of those suffering addictive or compulsive behaviors. The concept is simple, that lost and broken people can make a home for each other by offering solace, hope, and support, simply by sharing their own experiences as they try to grow spiritually.

The fellowships are based on the original principles of the twelve steps that Alcoholics Anonymous calls its program of recovery:

1. We admitted we were powerless over alcohol—that our lives had become unmanageable.
2. Came to believe that a Power greater than ourselves could restore us to sanity.
3. Made a decision to turn our will and our lives over to the care of God *as we understood Him.*
4. Made a searching and fearless moral inventory of ourselves.
5. Admitted to God, to ourselves and to another human being the exact nature of our wrongs.
6. Were entirely ready to have God remove all these defects of character.
7. Humbly asked Him to remove our shortcomings.
8. Made a list of all persons we had harmed, and became willing to make amends to them all.
9. Made direct amends to such people wherever possible, except when to do so would injure them or others.
10. Continued to take personal inventory and when we were wrong promptly admitted it.
11. Sought through prayer and meditation to improve our conscious contact with God, *as we understood Him,* praying only for knowledge of His will for us and the power to carry that out.
12. Having had a spiritual awakening as a result of these steps, we tried to carry this message to alcoholics, and to practice these principles in all our affairs.

The Twelve Steps are reprinted with permission of Alcoholics Anonymous World Services, Inc. Permission to reprint the Twelve Steps does not mean that A.A. has reviewed or approved the contents of this publication, nor that A.A. agrees with the views expressed herein. A.A. is a program of recovery from alcoholism *only*—use of the Twelve Steps in connection with programs and activities which are patterned after A.A., but which address other problems, does not imply otherwise.

The wording in these twelve suggestions is quite deliberate. It provides a path, or personal discipline, by which a person can grow without judgment. Sharp-eyed readers will note the important components of these steps. First of all, the steps begin with "we" because community is essential to the healing process. Changing within a community challenges the outsider feeling of alcoholics, addicts, and other compulsive persons who live in spiritual and emotional isolation. To grow—in other words, to be in the process of recovery—these people must learn to turn around their long-standing habit of going it alone and must face the shame, fear, and unworthiness they feel when they depend on self-destructive behavior as their comforter, friend, and lover.

A short prayer, known as the Serenity Prayer, may begin or end each meeting of twelve-step groups. Taken from a longer prayer penned by theologian Reinhold Niebuhr, it says, "God, grant me the serenity to accept the things I cannot change, the courage to change the things I can, and the wisdom to know the difference." With these words, the speaker is reminded of the detachment necessary to take responsibility for life without being responsible for controlling it.

Members of twelve-step groups are encouraged to develop a willingness to be open to spiritual experiences. The "big book," the text of Alcoholics Anonymous, asserts that group members must develop a spiritual basis for their lives. There is no dogma, and no one imposes beliefs about a higher power to anyone else. Individuals are left to discover and name their higher power for themselves. Some people return to their childhood religion with a fresh eye; others shop for a religious denomination that is appropriate to their changing beliefs. For others, it is the power of the group that is the power greater than the individual. But a growing sense of spirituality results from an ongoing search for a personal experience of a higher power, an experience available to each recovering person in times of pain, confusion, and temptation.

Also important is the concept of anonymity. During meetings, members identify themselves by first names only. Originally meant to serve as a protection from gossip, this tradition encourages members to share painful secrets, vulnerabilities, and struggles, and to know that what they share will never be repeated. Anonymity also assures that there is no hierarchy in the organization. Everyone, newcomer and veteran alike, is equal in the fellowship, and members take turns in chairing the meetings. Each person is aware that he or she is always growing, always developing, always vulnerable to the temptation of returning to any number of self-destructive behavior patterns. Anonymity undermines the operation of the ego so that singleness of purpose, that is, the maintenance of physical sobriety or emotional balance, keeps the focus on the spiritual path rather than on power struggles or personal gain.

The sacramental center is the meeting itself. With prayer, announcements, and a ritual reading of the twelve steps and twelve traditions, it contains familiar elements of a church service. But the core of each meeting is the storytelling. Members are encouraged to participate by telling about their own experience of recovery: how they once were, what happened to them, and what they are like today.

When speaking, participants are urged to talk from direct experience rather than from dogmatic belief. Those who attend have an opportunity to articulate a piece of their individual life journey, as they tell and retell their stories. A story may shift as the person grows and changes, gains new insights, recovers painful memories, explores new struggles. The use of a sponsor—a kind of mentor in the program who listens and guides whenever called upon—gives support to new members as they work the steps, examining their relationships with their past, exploring their limitations, and listing their assets.

In the best meetings, the community remains nonjudgmental. Members do not interrupt or give advice or mandates. They simply own their individual experiences and offer suggestions for recovery that have worked for them. New members are invited to try these suggestions and check their experience to determine if alternate behaviors offer relief from their past unmanageable conduct. Veterans then listen and tell each newcomer to "take what you like and leave the rest" and "keep coming back." The sharing of experience creates a significant emotional bond, and as that bond develops, the act of attendance shifts from that of an obligation to a source of strength.

Does it work? Does the twelve-step program get results? Millions of people, describing themselves as hopeless alcoholics or addicts, tell their stories daily of near ruin and personal disaster. They tell of automobiles tipping dangerously over cliffs, of incapacitating brain damage and physical illness, and of failing marriages, lost fortunes, and deteriorating families. As noted earlier, many have adapted the steps to help them look inward, to attend to other serious life concerns. Although each member is personally responsible to work the steps in order to move ahead on the spiritual path, the companionship of the fellowship supports people in this work.

There are some who believe that the twelve-step movement will one day revolutionize psychiatry, mental health, and pastoral counseling. Certainly it will be helpful to churches if their members and the clergy gain an understanding of how alcoholism, addiction, and dysfunction damage family life and prevent its members from intimacy with self, others, and a spiritual Presence.

There are elements of the twelve-step model that can serve as a paradigm for other communities of personal support. For example, it teaches us that any community is built out of the opportunity for and willingness of people to tell their stories. Telling our stories means that we are willing to be vulnerable, to reveal our struggles and doubts, our limitations and failures as well as our triumphs and strengths. Vulnerability comes in different forms, but clearly community can occur only when we are willing to risk being honest with our feelings, meanings, and thoughts in the presence of others. The atmosphere for safety necessary for such openness to occur comes only when such vulnerability is seen by the other people in community as strength rather than as weakness. When Jesus knelt to wash the feet of his disciples, he demonstrated the vulnerability that is the hallmark of the leadership style necessary for true community. When churches follow the pattern of most business institutions and adopt a leadership of privilege, then community is sacrificed. Jesus contrasted the community of his followers with the typical leadership of his day by telling his disciples that those who would be great among them must be servants to all. In other words, vulnerability is the prerequisite to leadership.

In the church, the price we pay for the scarcity of trust in the power of vulnerability is a lack of openness and sincerity. Concepts such as forgiveness, grace, and faith become mere words without the support of experience. They lack meaning when they are not grounded in the lives of people. But when attached to the struggles and transformations of human beings, these concepts can be powerful experiences. However, we can witness the reality of such connections only as we tell our stories in the presence of others and listen to the stories of others.

M. Scott Peck describes four stages in the development of community.[30] The first is a period of pseudocommunity, a stage when members attempt to fake community by avoiding disagreements, minimizing differences, and emphasizing pleasantness. In this stage, effort is made to avoid conflict rather than resolve it.

The second stage is that of chaos, a time in which individual differences come forth with a vengeance. It is a time of much struggle and tension because every effort is made to obliterate differences and to try to heal or convert others.[31]

The third stage is one of emptiness. It is the stage of letting go of preconceived ideas and expectations that we may bring to the group process. It is also a time for letting go of the effort, subtle as it may be, to change or fix others. This is often the time when group members begin to share more openly their failures and fears, their doubts and defeats. And in the final stage, community can come with a dynamic silence, as new life emerges from the emptiness and a place of safety is created.

Those who successfully come into an experience of community move beyond helpfulness, are able to be a nonanxious presence in the face of others' hurts and struggles, and are vulnerable to themselves and others.

A remarkable experience that comes with entering deeply into our own inward being and with developing a healthy self-love is that we discover that "solidarity is the other side of intimacy."[32] Solidarity with others might best be described in the words of scientist-priest Pierre Teilhard de Chardin, as a "conspiracy of love."[33] Since "to conspire" literally means "to breathe together,"[34] it conveys an intimate joining with others in their struggle to achieve identity and empowerment. In its deepest sense, intimacy causes us to recognize the interconnectedness of all life.

Intimacy cannot be privatized or confined only to those with whom we have much in common. It pushes our boundaries out to include even those with whom we may have great differences. When Jesus was once invited to a prestigious dinner, he daringly said to his host: "When you give a luncheon or a dinner, do not invite your friends . . . your relatives or rich neighbors." In other words, do not invite those who can repay with a return invitation, but rather "invite the poor, the crippled, the lame and the blind,"[35] those who cannot reciprocate the favor. These words invite us to move beyond the bounds of the familiar to an inclusive attitude, to intimate communion with all humanity.

In the long run, this is an invitation to experience the intimate nature of the universe. We recognize the truth in the words of Henri Nouwen, which head this chapter: "The closer we come to the heart of the One who loves us with an unconditional love, the closer we come to each other in the solidarity of a redeemed humanity."[36] It is for this that, in Paul's beautiful and prophetic words, "the creation waits with eager longing."[37]

Notes

Chapter 1—Search for Intimacy

1. Martin Buber, *I and Thou*, 2d ed. (New York: Charles Scribner's Sons, 1958), 11.
2. Thomas Patrick Malone, M.D., and Patrick Thomas Malone, M.D., *The Art of Intimacy* (New York: Prentice Hall, 1987), 19.
3. Lillian B. Rubin, *Intimate Strangers: Men and Women Together* (New York: Harper & Row, 1983), 79.
4. John Welwood, *Journey of the Heart: Intimate Relationship and the Path of Love* (New York: HarperCollins, 1990), 1-2.
5. Martin Buber, "Distance and Relation," *Psychiatry: Journal for the Study of Interpersonal Process* 20 (May 1957): 97-113.
6. Gerald G. May, M.D., *Will and Spirit: A Contemplative Psychology* (New York: Harper & Row, 1983), 5-7.
7. Welwood, *Journey of the Heart*, 92.
8. Jordan Paul and Margaret Paul, *Do I Have to Give Up Me to Be Loved by You?* (Minneapolis: CompCare, 1983), 5-10.
9. Rainer Maria Rilke, *Letters to a Young Poet* (New York: W. W. Norton & Co., 1962), 35.
10. Erik H. Erikson, *Childhood and Society*, 2d ed. (New York: W. W. Norton & Co., 1963), 263.
11. Evelyn Eaton Whitehead and James D. Whitehead, *Christian Life Patterns: The Psychological Challenges and Religions Invitations of Adult Life* (Garden City, N.Y.: Doubleday, 1982), 80.

Chapter 2—Fearful Intimacy

1. Henri J. M. Nouwen, *Lifesigns: Intimacy, Fecundity, and Ecstasy in Christian Perspective* (Garden City, N.Y.: Doubleday, 1986), 30.
2. Welwood, *Journey of the Heart*, 104.
3. Nouwen, *Lifesigns*, 30-31.

4. Ibid., 31.

5. Sam Keen, *Faces of the Enemy: Reflections of the Hostile Imagination* (San Francisco: Harper & Row, 1986), 18.

6. Ibid., 25.

7. Nouwen, *Lifesigns*, 31.

8. Paul Tillich, *The Courage to Be*, Terry Lecture Series (New Haven, Conn.: Yale Univ. Press, 1952), 89. Tillich describes "individualization" and "participation" as the first polar elements in the structure of being. These terms carry much of the meaning I am attaching to "distance" and "closeness."

9. Harriet Goldhor Lerner, *The Dance of Intimacy* (New York: Harper & Row, 1989), 9.

10. Harville Hendrix, *Getting the Love You Want* (New York: Henry Holt, 1988), 107.

11. Lillian Rubin in her book *Intimate Strangers* uses the term "approach-avoidance dance."

12. Ellyn Bader and Peter T. Pearson, *In Quest of the Mythical Mate* (New York: Brunner/Mazel Publishers, 1988), 4-9. Bader and Pearson give an excellent synopsis of Margaret Mahler's model of childhood development and correlate it to the stages of couples' relationships.

13. Mahler, Pine, and Bergman quoted in Bader and Pearson, *In Quest of the Mythical Mate*, 5.

14. Hendrix, *Getting the Love You Want*, 17.

15. Ibid., 18.

16. Bader and Pearson, *In Quest of the Mythical Mate*, 7.

17. Ibid., 7.

18. Hendrix, *Getting the Love You Want*, 15.

19. Ibid., 15.

20. Bader and Pearson, *In Quest of the Mythical Mate*, 63-66. I owe much to Bader and Pearson's characterization of the symbiotic-symbiotic couple, which is the best description I have seen of the fearful closeness in couple relationships.

21. Kahlil Gibran, *The Prophet* (New York: Alfred A. Knopf, 1951).

22. Tillich, *The Courage to Be*, 86-89.

23. Nouwen, *Lifesigns*, 36.

24. Ibid., 147. I am grateful to William Johnston who in his book *Silent Music* makes the distinction between "merging" and "indwelling." As I understand these terms, merging involves the loss of separate identity, the loss of "I" in the "we." Indwelling retains, even expands, the "I" in the experience of the "we."

25. John 15:4.

26. William Johnston, *Silent Music: The Science of Meditation* (New York: Harper & Row, 1974), 148.

Chapter 3—Escapes from Intimacy

1. Robert Laing quoted in Claude M. Steiner, *Scripts People Live* (New York: Bantam Books, 1975), 72-74.

2. Fanita English, "The Substitution Factor: Rackets and Real Feelings (Part 1)," *Transactional Analysis Journal* 1, no. 4 (Oct. 1971): 25-26.

3. Hendrix, *Getting the Love You Want*, 24-25.

4. Welwood, *Journey of the Heart*, 16.

5. Robert Goulding, "Decisions in Script Formation," *Transactional Analysis Journal* 2, no. 2 (April 1972): 62-63.

6. Rubin, *Intimate Strangers*, 90.

7. Ibid., 91.

8. Luke 10:40.

9. Mark 14:34.

10. John 5:2-9.

11. Romans 7:19.

12. Romans 7:20.

13. Welwood, *Journey of the Heart*, 18.

14. Hendrix, *Getting the Love You Want*, 68.

15. Ibid., 69.

16. Ibid., 77–78.

17. Welwood, *Journey of the Heart*, 120.

18. Ibid.

19. Luke 6:41.

20. Ephesians 4:15.

21. Joseph Campbell, *The Power of Myth: Joseph Campbell with Bill Moyers*, ed. Betty Sue Flowers (New York: Doubleday, 1988), 117.

Chapter 4—Expressions of Intimacy

1. Welwood, *Journey of the Heart*, 1.

2. M. Scott Peck, *The Road Less Traveled: A New Psychology of Love, Traditional Values and Spiritual Growth*, 2d ed. (New York: Simon & Schuster, 1978), 87.

3. Welwood, *Journey of the Heart*, 89.

4. I am indebted to Steve Karpman for this insight.

5. Hendrix, *Getting the Love You Want*, 139–40.

6. Welwood, *Journey of the Heart*, 92.

7. Paul and Paul, *Do I Have to Give Up Me to Be Loved by You?* 49.

8. Ibid.

9. Rubin, *Intimate Strangers*, 69.

10. Ibid., 71.

11. Sam Keen, *Fire in the Belly: On Being a Man* (New York: Bantam, 1990), 214.

12. Ibid.

13. Maggie Scarf, *Intimate Partners: Patterns in Love and Marriage* (New York: Ballantine Books, 1988), 151.

14. Howard J. Clinebell, Jr., and Charlotte H. Clinebell, *The Intimate Marriage* (New York: Harper & Row, 1970), 28–32.

15. Erikson, *Childhood and Society*, 267.
16. Clinebell and Clinebell, *The Intimate Marriage*, 30.
17. Quoted in John Welwood, *Journey of the Heart*, 172-73.
18. Clinebell and Clinebell, *The Intimate Marriage*, 179.
19. 1 John 4:7-8.

Chapter 5—Making Life Connections

1. Erich Fromm, *The Art of Loving: Intimate Relationship and the Path of Love* (New York: Harper & Row, 1956), 22.
2. Peck, *The Road Less Traveled*, 81.
3. Buber, *I and Thou*, 75.
4. Mark 12:30-31.
5. James Hillman, *Insearch: Psychology and Religion* (New York: Charles Scribner's Sons, 1967), 37.
6. Fromm, *The Art of Loving*, 51.
7. Ibid., 33.
8. Hendrix, *Getting the Love You Want*, 20.
9. Ibid., 17.
10. 1 John 4:16.
11. Paul Tournier, *The Meaning of Persons* (New York: Harper & Row, 1957), 13.
12. Keen, *Fire in the Belly*, 219.
13. Malone, and Malone, *The Art of Intimacy*, 263.
14. Ibid., 265.
15. Ibid.
16. Ibid., 263.
17. Matthew 19:16-21.
18. The word *perfect* is a translation of the Greek *teleos*, meaning to be complete.

19. Matthew 23:27.
20. Rainer Maria Rilke, *Letters to a Young Poet*, rev. ed., trans. M. D. Herter Norton (New York: W. W. Norton & Co., 1954), 18-19.
21. Henri J. M. Nouwen, *Reaching Out: The Three Movements of the Spiritual Life* (Garden City, N.Y.: Doubleday & Company, 1975), 26.
22. Keen, *Fire in the Belly*, 161.
23. Ibid.
24. Nouwen, *Reaching Out*, 25.
25. Keen, *Fire in the Belly*, 161.
26. Lerner, *The Dance of Intimacy*, 105.
27. Quoted in Elizabeth O'Connor, *Our Many Selves: A Handbook for Self-Discovery* (New York: Harper & Row, 1971), 39.
28. *The Interpreter's Dictionary of the Bible*, vol. 4, ed. George Arthur Buttrick (New York: Abingdon Press, 1962), 3.
29. Carl Jung, *Psychology and Religion: West and East*, trans. R. F. C. Hull (Princeton, N.J.: Princeton University Press, 1969), 339.
30. Fromm, *The Art of Loving*, 49.
31. Welwood, *Journey of the Heart*, 89.
32. Gabriel Marcel, *The Philosophy of Existence* (New York: Books for Libraries, 1949), 25.
33. Marsha Sinetar, *Elegant Choices, Healing Choices* (New York: Paulist Press, 1988), 33.
34. Nouwen, *Reaching Out*, 47.
35. Marilyn Ferguson, *The Aquarian Conspiracy* (Los Angeles: J. P. Tarcher, 1980), 145.
36. Quoted in Johnston, *Silent Music*, 92.
37. Ibid., 161.
38. William Barrett, *Irrational Man: A Study in Existential Philosophy* (Garden City, N.Y.: Doubleday, 1958), 73.
39. Ibid., 74.
40. Ibid.

41. John Amodeo and Kris Wentworth, *Being Intimate: A Guide to Successful Relationships* (London: Penguin Group, 1986), 100.

42. Barret, *Irrational Man*, 74.

43. Job 42:5.

44. Johnston, *Silent Music*, 147.

45. John 15:4.

46. Johnston, *Silent Music*, 147.

47. Tilden Edwards *Living in the Presence* (New York: Harper & Row, 1987), 2. Edwards defines spiritual formation as all those mysterious ways that God seeks to form us in God's likeness through all dimensions of our individual and corporate lives.

Chapter 6—Building Communities of Personal Support

1. Nouwen, *Lifesigns*, 28-29.

2. Robert N. Bellah et al., *Habits of the Heart: Individualism and Communism in American Life* (Berkeley: University of California Press, 1985), 232.

3. According to sociologist Wade Clark Roof in a study funded by the Lilly Endowment Fund, "At one time or another, roughly two thirds of baby boomers dropped out of organized religion. But in recent years, more than one third of the dropouts have returned." Quoted in *Newsweek*, 17 Dec. 1990, 51.

4. The book by Edwin H. Friedman, *Generation to Generation: Family Process in Church and Synagogue* (New York: The Guilford Press, 1985) is an excellent resource for relating family theory to the context of religious community.

5. Buber, *I and Thou*, 11.

6. Luke 18:11.

7. M. Scott Peck, M.D., *The Different Drum: Community Making and Peace* (New York: Simon & Schuster, 1987), 61.

8. Harold S. Kushner, *Who Needs God* (New York: Summit Books, 1989), 110-11.

9. Campbell, *The Power of Myth*, 61.

10. Larry Dossey, M.D., *Recovering the Soul: A Scientific and Spiritual Search* (New York: Bantam Books, 1989), 60.

11. An excellent resource on this understanding of prayer is by Ann Ulanov and Barry Ulanov, *Primary Speech: A Psychology of Prayer* (Atlanta: John Knox Press, 1982).

12. Malone and Malone, *The Art of Intimacy*, 2.

13. Peck, *The Different Drum*, 59.

14. Ibid., 25.

15. Ibid., 61-62.

16. Amodeo and Wentworth, *Being Intimate*, 110.

17. Ibid., 111.

18. Ibid.

19. Ibid., 121.

20. Peck, *The Different Drum*, 71.

21. Amodeo and Wentworth, *Being Intimate*, 194.

22. Peck, *The Different Drum*, 97.

23. Ibid.

24. Friedman, *Generation to Generation*, 208-10.

25. Ibid., 209.

26. Ibid., 50.

27. Ibid., 51.

28. Ibid., 57.

29. Matthew 7:3.

30. Peck, *The Different Drum*, 86-106.

31. Ibid., 91.

32. Nouwen, *Lifesigns*, 43.

33. Quoted in Ferguson, *The Aquarian Conspiracy*, 19.

34. Ibid.

35. Luke 14:12ff.

36. Nouwen, *Lifesigns*, 51.

37. Romans 8:19.

Selected Bibliography

Amodeo, John, and Kris Wentworth. *Being Intimate: A Guide to Successful Relationships*. London: Penguin Group, 1986.

Buber, Martin. *I and Thou*. 2d ed. New York: Charles Scribner's Sons, 1958.

Clinebell, Howard J., Jr., and Charlotte H. Clinebell. *The Intimate Marriage*. New York: Harper & Row, 1970.

Edwards, Tilden. *Living in the Presence*. New York: Harper & Row, 1987.

Johnston, William. *Silent Music: The Science of Meditation*. New York: Harper & Row, 1976.

Malone, Thomas Patrick, M.D., and Patrick Thomas Malone, M.D. *The Art of Intimacy*. New York: Prentice-Hall, 1987.

Nouwen, Henri J. M. *Lifesigns: Intimacy, Fecundity, and Ecstasy in Christian Perspective*. New York: Doubleday, 1986.

Peck, M. Scott, M.D., *The Different Drum: Community Making and Peace*. New York: Simon & Schuster, 1987.

Ulanov, Ann, and Barry Ulanov. *Primary Speech: A Psychology of Prayer*. Atlanta: John Knox Press, 1982.

Welwood, John. *Journey of The Heart: Intimate Relationship and the Path of Love*. New York: HarperCollins, 1990.

Intimacy

The Quest for Life Connections

Leader's Guide

James W. Hanna

A Kaleidoscope Series Resource

United Church Press
Cleveland, Ohio

Objectives of the Course

Each person who completes this course will be able—
1. To understand the meaning of intimacy in relating to self, others, the created order, and God;
2. To explain the dynamics of intimate relationships;
3. To expand personal capacity for establishing intimate relationships and to experience and express intimacy;
4. To identify ways of creating communities of personal support.

Although the aim of this course is educational rather than therapeutic, the nature of the topic and the format of the class may require a level of introspection and mutual sharing that is unfamiliar and even uncomfortable for some participants. It is important for the leader, therefore, to respect the limits of each class member by inviting but not insisting on participation. During the various exercises and activities, each participant should be given permission to share to the degree he or she desires.

Learning and Leadership Style

This guide makes the following assumptions:
1. The leader for this course does not need to be a professional teacher or counselor. Nevertheless, he or she should be nonjudgmental in leading the discussions and able to express views without imposing them on others.
2. The leader is expected to have read the text in advance of the class and be familiar with the subjects covered.
3. Class participants should keep a journal throughout the class, entering significant insights they have during the various exercises as well as those gained between class times.
4. Since continuity is essential for the course, class members should be encouraged to attend all sessions, to read the assignments in advance of each class, and to keep a record of their reflections on the reading, especially on the case illustrations (the stories of people in therapy).

Time, Space, and Equipment

This course is designed for six two-hour sessions with time needed between each class for assignments.

The class will need to break down into small discussion groups from time to time, so the meeting space should be large enough to accommodate small groups, and the furniture should be movable. A chalkboard and chalk, or a large newsprint easel and several markers are necessary. You will also need wall space to hang newspaper and magazine clippings.

A VCR-VHS system is necessary to show the videocassette tape that accompanies this course. Whoever operates the video equipment should be familiar with the system before the class begins.

Educational Components

Each session gives a suggested teaching process. In general, you as leader will have to decide on the amount of time to allot to the various numbered components and exercises, based on scheduling needs and interests of the class participants.

Depending on the size of the class, decide on the time needed for breaking the group into smaller groups. If the group consists of less than ten members, it may be best to remain together for some of the discussions. You are encouraged, however, to keep the groups smaller for the exercises and personal sharing.

A fifteen-minute break (ideally with refreshments) is important to schedule during the two-hour session. A partner back rub, with the group standing in a circle and gently rubbing the shoulders and back of the person in front and then reversing the circle, can be a way of keeping the group energetic.

Since some of the case illustrations may require more reflection than other parts of the book, it may be important to ask the participants to spend some time reflecting on these cases in particular in advance of the class session.

Because the smaller cluster groups are often asked to discuss questions, have these questions printed beforehand on newsprint.

Throughout the Leader's Guide there are notes by the author headed "Comments." These explanations are intended as background information for you as leader and may be used for introducing a discussion or for the exercises, as appropriate.

Each session should begin with an appropriate prayer and reading. It may be beneficial to have various class members share readings related to the issue of intimacy that they have found helpful.

At the end of each session there are suggested questions for the class to consider in preparation for the following session. Prepare these as handouts to be given to class members at the end of the session.

Participants should read the first chapter of the book prior to the first group meeting.

Chapter 1: Search for Intimacy

Objectives

1. To create a relaxed atmosphere in which all participants feel invited to be candid and feel safe in expressing their thoughts and feelings.

2. To state the objectives, style, and expectations of the course.

3. To introduce on videotape the author, who will assist in the initiation of the course.

4. To explore some cultural and personal understandings of intimacy.

Suggested Teaching Process

Advanced Preparation. Gather several examples from newspapers or magazines of items, including advertisements, that illustrate our culture's image of intimacy and intimate relationships. Members of the class may be invited to glean such illustrations prior to the first meeting. Several of these may be posted on a bulletin board. If time permits, you may want to make a videocassette tape of several television advertisements or gather examples from popular music that exemplify the theme of intimacy. Prepare a sheet of newsprint as suggested in activity 7.

1. Open the session with a prayer and Bible reading, poem, or other reading on the subject of intimacy.

Comment: How we introduce ourselves to others is an important part of establishing our boundaries of self-disclosure; it contains a message to others regarding how and to what extent we wish to be known.

2. Ask each person to give his or her name and one "important" piece of information about him- or herself.

Comment: It is important initially to be aware of the assumptions the group brings to the concept of intimacy.

3. Divide the group into clusters of no more than four persons. Ask the participants each to: "Picture in your mind a concrete scene

or an episode in which you experienced intimacy, perhaps with another person, with a group, with nature." After giving a few minutes for each person to clarify his or her mental picture, say: "Share briefly your experience of intimacy with your cluster. What were some of its characteristics?"

4. Write the word *intimacy* on the top of a sheet of newsprint or a chalkboard. Reassemble the entire group in front of the word. Ask the group: "When you hear the word *intimacy*, what single word immediately comes to your mind?" List the various words contributed by the group, writing them on the newsprint, but avoiding any comment at this point. Emphasize to the group that it is important to speak the words that immediately come to mind and to avoid comment as people speak.

5. Ask each person to consider the list that has been presented and his or her own personal experience and to write on a sheet of paper a single sentence defining intimacy. Emphasize to the group that defining intimacy is not a substitute for the experience of intimacy ("the map is not the trip"), but our definitions can help clarify the experience. State that the group will have the opportunity to revise their definitions as the course progresses. You may want to ask at this point if a few people want to share their definitions. These should simply be reported and not discussed in detail at this point.

6. Play video segment 1A, in which the author introduces the course. At the end of the segment, present an overview of the course, emphasizing that this course will focus both on understanding and increasing our capacity for experiencing intimacy in all dimensions of our lives. The following items, which you have listed on newsprint, should also be presented:

a) An outline of the course objectives

b) The learning styles of the course and the expectations of the leader

7. State to the group that it is time to move beyond definitions of intimacy to images, which are far more powerful in determining and relating our views on intimacy.

8. Again arrange the group into clusters of four persons. (These can be the same cluster groups formed for the earlier discussion.) Play video segment 1B, in which a small group is interviewed regarding their images of intimacy. Ask your groups to watch for

various cultural images expressed by those being interviewed.

9. Following the video review, ask each cluster to peruse the various magazine and newspaper selections posted on the bulletin board. If you have prerecorded television advertisements or selections from popular music, play these at this point. Ask the participants to reflect on ideas and images regarding intimacy that they receive from movies, plays, television series, or popular music. Ask each group to consider these questions: "What do you believe are the main characteristics of our cultural image of intimacy as presented in the media?" "What do you think of the image of the 'perfect fit'?"

10. Reassemble as an entire group. Ask each cluster to report on the characteristics of our culture's image of intimacy that they discerned. List the characteristics on the newsprint.

11. List the three polarities of distance and closeness, power and cooperation, giving and receiving, as elements that comprise the experience of intimacy. Ask the group to share from their reading their understanding of these three contrasting movements of relationships.

12. Again, divide into clusters, appointing a member of the group as convener for each cluster. Assign each group one of the three vignettes presented in the text. (Participants may choose to cluster according to the vignette that appeals to them most.) Ask each cluster to consider and discuss how polarity—distance/closeness, power/cooperation, giving/receiving—affects the relationship of the people in the vignette.

13. Reassemble in the larger group and discuss briefly the need to balance each of the polarities. (Each is a gift, but each can also hinder intimacy when it is not balanced by the other dynamic.)

14. Write the following Evelyn and James Whitehead quotation on newsprint: "A well-developed capacity for intimacy enables a person to honor the promises and demands of commitment and to sustain with integrity the adjustments and compromises required in living with others." Ask the group: "What part do you believe commitment plays in our capacity for being intimate with ourselves and with others?" Ask each group member to consider silently what level of commitment she or he has to develop a personal capacity for being intimate in relating to self and others.

Suggested Questions to Consider for Session 2

Comment: Chapter 2 focuses on the various fears that impact on our effort at creating intimate relationships. It would be helpful to have the group reflect on some common fears that they have regarding relationships.

1. List in your journal some common fears that you and other people you know may have, such as rejection. How many of your fears have to do with relationships—with yourself and with others?

2. What are some of the ways you tend to distance yourself in relationships? What ways do you seek closeness?

Chapter 2: Fearful Intimacy

Objectives

1. To identify fears that affect our ability to be intimate with self and others.

2. To discern social and personal expressions of fearful distance and fearful closeness as ways of avoiding intimacy.

Suggested Teaching Process

1. Open with a prayer and an appropriate reading relating to fear and intimacy.

Comment: "Fear is the great enemy of intimacy," according to writer and theologian Henri Nouwen. The second session will focus on the underlying fears that disrupt our ability to be intimate.

2. Write Nouwen's quotation above on newsprint. While remaining in the larger group, ask the members to list fears, which they have written in their journals, that they believe affect people's capacity for intimate relationships. After the group has an adequate opportunity to contribute, inquire whether they see common themes among the various fears listed. Remind the group that psychologist John Welwood writes, "At the core of all fears of intimacy is a fear of loss"—the fear of the loss of love (such as being left alone or abandoned) or the fear of the loss of self (such as being engulfed or emotionally controlled).

3. Ask the group to consider the list again, marking each item with either an A for fear of loss of love or a B for fear of loss of self.

4. List the phrases "Fearful Distance" and "Fearful Closeness" on separate sheets of newsprint. Ask the group to share what they have

learned from their reading regarding these two concepts. Emphasize the distinction of these terms from the primary healthy tendencies of closeness and distance, which are a part of all relating.

5. Divide the group into clusters of four. Play video segment 2A, which focuses on social situations in which people experience fearful distancing and closeness. Ask members to watch for characteristics of social distancing and closeness. Following the video ask each cluster to consider social examples of fearful distance and fearful closeness in our society.

6. Remaining in clusters, play video segment 2B, which shows couples at various stages in their relationship discussing the dance of intimacy and the dynamic of closeness and distance in their relating. Ask participants to watch for the characteristics of distancing and closeness in these personal relationships.

7. Following the video ask each group to reflect on these questions: "In what particular ways do you create distance and closeness?" "What are some appropriate ways of creating distance and closeness?"

8. Close the session by gathering the group in a circle and inviting members to offer sentence prayers, particularly related to fears.

Suggested Questions to Consider for Session 3

Comment: Chapter 3 focuses on family messages that affect our ability to be intimate and on ways of relating that mask as intimacy but lack the mutuality and vulnerability characteristic of true intimacy.

1. Review your family's history regarding messages about relating to others by considering the following questions:

a) What feeling or feelings were most frequently expressed in your household?

b) How was anger viewed by your family?

c) Who was the person in your family you could most easily talk with about your feelings?

d) How was affection expressed? Was touch part of the way your family showed affection?

2. Read and reflect on the two models of relating in the New Testament mentioned in the chapter: Martha (Luke 10:38-42) and the invalid lying by the pool of Bethzatha (John 5:1-18). In what ways can you identify with each character? Enter you observations in your journal.

3. To the next session, bring a picture of yourself as a child, one that may have special meaning or special memories for you.

Chapter 3: Escapes from Intimacy
Objectives
1. To explore family messages regarding expression of feelings, needs, and thoughts.
2. To introduce familiar patterns of behavior that mask as intimacy.

Suggested Teaching Process
1. Open with prayer and an appropriate reading.
2. Divide the large group into clusters of four persons. Invite each to review the stories at the beginning of the chapter, of Lucie, Millie, Mary, Randy, Joe, and Julie, and to discuss ways that family messages are conveyed in each vignette.
3. Play video segment 3A, in which the author shows a picture of himself as a child and shares some information regarding himself and his mask of intimacy.
4. Following the video, remain in small groups. Have participants share the pictures of themselves that they brought and tell their cluster group a brief story associated with the picture.
5. Invite each person into a brief journey of fantasy into his or her past. Ask members to close their eyes in order to picture themselves in the setting of the home where they were raised. Invite them to visualize a scene involving members of their family and while doing so to reflect on the following questions:
   a) How were feelings of anger, sadness, joy, and fear expressed?
   b) What feelings were avoided?
   c) How did family members express their wants?

An alternative activity is the following exercise suggested by theologian and philosopher Sam Keen. Ask members to draw a floor plan of a home where they were raised. Divide the group into pairs and, using the drawing, ask each person to take his or her partner on a brief tour of the house. Suggest several areas that can be described by answering such questions as the following: "Where did people gather?" "Was there a place where you did not feel welcome?" "How did people interact in your family, for example, around the dinner table?" "How did family members avoid each other?" "How did family members express closeness?"

6. Introduce the two masks of intimacy presented in the chapter by writing the words "Caretaking" and "Dependency" on newsprint. Ask group members to list characteristics of each mask, and continue to emphasize that these are learned expressions of our need to make a connection with others by giving and receiving. Ask the group, "Which mask do you relate to the most?" Give examples.

7. Divide into cluster groups again, so that each can read and consider two biblical passages—Luke 10:38-42 and John 51-18—and one or two of the vignettes in the chapter, examples of intimacy masks. Ask each member to share which character he or she can identify with. Ask each group to consider the question "What does the character in each passage give up in pursuing his or her particular mask of intimacy?"

8. While the participants remain in cluster groups, list on newsprint the three ways, as presented by Harville Hendrix, in which our relationships confront us with disowned parts of ourselves. Ask each cluster to consider how the vignettes demonstrate these ways of disowning parts of ourselves. Ask each group to discuss how disowning part of ourselves affects our ability to be intimate with another. Ask, "What does it mean to follow your bliss?"

9. Close the session by gathering in a circle and inviting sentence prayers focused on our need to both give and receive.

Suggested Questions to Consider for Session 4

Comment: Chapter 4 focuses on the variety of ways that intimacy can be expressed. We will consider the contexts in which intimacy may occur in order to move beyond the stereotypes of the intimate experience.

1. How would you describe the difference between an intimate moment and an intimate relationship?

2. What are some of the situations in which you have experienced intimacy? Explore from your own life various kinds of intimacy that you have experienced: task-oriented, intellectual, emotional, physical, and so on.

Chapter 4: Expressions of Intimacy

Objectives
1. To define the difference between an intimate moment and an intimate experience.
2. To identify and illustrate various expressions of intimacy.

Suggested Teaching Process
   1. Open the session with prayer and an appropriate reading.

   Comment: Psychologist and author John Welwood describes times of mutual openness and inner sharing in relationships as "soul-connections." This session will focus on such experiences.

   2. Remind the group that people experience various kinds of intimacy. List on newsprint the kinds mentioned in the chapter: crisis intimacy (e.g., the incident of Jessica McClure), intellectual intimacy, physical intimacy, task-oriented intimacy, emotional intimacy. (We also experience intimate moments as well as intimate relationships.) Ask the group to give a brief example of each type of intimacy.

   3. Divide the group into clusters of four persons. Have each group reflect on the different ways they have experienced intimacy. Ask each participant to give specific examples of times he or she has experienced a soul connection. Discuss the variety of contexts in which these intimate experiences occurred. Ask, "Were these intimate moments or intimate relationships?"

   4. Play video segment 4, in which three individuals discuss specific experiences of intimacy. Ask the group to watch for differences and similarities of each individuals's description. In what ways do class participants identify with the experiences being shared on the video?

   Comment: Sharing emotions is a common ingredient in most definitions of intimacy. Emphasize to the group the significance of identifying our feelings in relating to others.

   5. Have each cluster group briefly list factors that prevent our awareness of feelings and expression of them. Ask each group to consider these questions: "What feelings do you find most difficult to express to other people or even to God?" "What feelings do you most frequently express?"

   6. Using the personal stories of people in therapy from the

chapter, introduce to the group the concept of containment and expression of feelings. Write the words of Ecclesiastes "A time to keep silence, and a time to speak" on newsprint. Ask each cluster group to consider these questions: "What do you see as the differences between denial of feelings and containment of feelings?" "When do you think it is most appropriate to contain feelings in relating to others?" "When is it important to express feelings?"

7. Close the session with a time of silence, inviting each person to reflect on moments of soul connection as channels of divine presence.

Suggested Questions to Consider for Session 5

Comment: Chapter 5 presents the importance of making an inner connection with our own feelings, thoughts, and beliefs as a prerequisite to connecting with others.

1. List in your journal some of the common barriers you find to a healthy sense of self-love.

2. How would you define the difference between selfishness and self-love?

3. Journalize specific events or relationships in your life that symbolize intimate connections. Record two or three specific memories of these connections.

Chapter 5: Making Life Connections

Objectives
1. To identify elements of a healthy sense of self-love.
2. To introduce the dynamics of making an intimate connection with other persons, with the created order, and with the Eternal.

Suggested Teaching Process
1. Open the session with prayer and a reading focused on the theme of love.

2. Write on newsprint the following definitions of love.

   Erich Fromm: "Love is the active concern for the life and the growth of that which we love."

   M. Scott Peck: "Love is . . . the will to extend one's self for the purpose of nurturing one's own or another's spiritual growth."

Ask the larger group to reflect on these definitions. Then ask "Are there common elements in both definitions?" "Do these definitions describe your experience of love?" "How would you expand these definitions?"

3. Divide into cluster groups of four. Invite each group to consider Jesus' words "You shall love your neighbor as yourself." Ask: "How do you believe loving yourself affects your ability to love others?" "What are the qualities of a healthy self-love?"

4. Reassemble in the larger group. Use the biblical stories and the contemporary accounts from chapter 5 in introducing the four ways of making a connection with ourselves presented by Sam Keen. List his ways on newsprint: (a) respectfully listening; (b) recollecting our experience; (c) cherishing paradox; (d) loving what we cannot understand. Divide into clusters. Ask the groups to reflect on this question: "How do Keen's four concepts compare to the qualities of healthy self-love that emerged in your discussions?" "How is self-love illustrated in the story of Sarah the architect?"

Comment: Making intimate connection with others has been characterized by psychiatrists Thomas and Patrick Malone as being "in your own personal space while you are also in the space you share with another."

5. Write the Malone quotation above on newsprint. Ask the group to briefly reflect on what it means to be in personal space while at the same time sharing space with another. Then ask, "How does this relate to dependence, independence, and interdependence?"

Comment: In Chapter 5 the author writes: "The story of our lives is framed within selected memories of our past experience. . . . They define for us who we are and who are the significant people in our lives."

6. Divide into cluster groups of four. Ask the group members to share one significant memory of an intimate connection from their growing up. Ask: "Who was involved?" "How was intimacy expressed?" "How has this memory affected your life?"

7. Play video segment 5A, which is a minilecture by the author on making life connections. Ask the group to listen for specific ways connections can be made. Ask, "How does the idea of 'sharing space with another' apply to our relationship with the created order?" Read a brief passage from one of the essays by anthropologist Loren Eiseley, or other such author, to use in

thinking about a relationship with nature as an expression of intimacy.

Comment: Writers Martin Buber and William Johnston have suggested that when we enter into an I-Thou relationship with another person or with nature, we open our hearts to experience the Eternal.

8. Play video segment 5B, in which two spiritual directors are interviewed regarding intimacy with God. Ask the group to listen for ways that an intimate connection with God is discovered. Ask the groups to consider these questions: "In what sense can we experience intimacy with God?" "Have you experienced the Eternal when you were relating to another person?" "Would you describe Job's relationship to God as intimate?"

9. Close by reading the Twenty-third Psalm, inviting group members to insert their names in place of the pronouns; for example, "... though I, ___ , walk through the darkest valley ... you are with me." Invite group members to recall times of intimate relating to others or to the created order, when God was present, and to offer brief sentence prayers giving thanks for such moments of presence.

Suggested Questions to Consider for Session 6

Comment: Robert Bellah and his colleagues have emphasized that most local churches define themselves as communities of personal support. Chapter 6 focuses on the church as an intimate community.

1. List in your journal words you associate with the image of home. What words do you associate with the image of church. Are your associations similar? How are they different?

2. Reflect on your last experience of communion. How did you feel connected with the other participants?

3. Reflect on a group experience of intimacy you had. Describe it.

Chapter 6:
Building Communities of Personal Support

Objectives
1. To define the attributes of true community.
2. To present communion as a symbol of intimacy.
3. To introduce the twelve-step program as a structure of intimate community.

Suggested Teaching Process

1. Open with a prayer and an appropriate reading.
2. Ask the group to list attributes which they associate with the image of home. Discuss the archetype of home as a symbol of community.
3. Divide the group into clusters of four people. Ask members to share with one another an experience of community. This experience may have been with a group of friends, people working on a common project, a group of colleagues, etc. Ask members also to describe how their particular community balanced the need for autonomy with the need for togetherness.
4. Invite the clusters to reflect on the story of Bruce in chapter 6: "How does Bruce's situation with his friends illustrate the dynamics of exclusive groups?" "Are you presently a part of an exclusive group?" "Are there times when exclusiveness is important to group survival?"
5. Gather in the larger group. Play video segment 6A, which is an interview with clergy and laypersons and is focused on the question "Where do people find community in the church?" Ask the class to listen for specific ways community is defined in the church. Following the video, ask, "How do we recognize true community?" List on newsprint the characteristics of true community outlined in the chapter: (a) "True community is inclusive, always seeking to expand itself"; (b) "Confrontation and conflict in community . . . provide an opportunity for people to expand their perspectives and to confront their differences"; (c) "The quest for true community . . . leads us beyond helpfulness." Ask, "What would a church look like that would have these characteristics?"

Comment: Therapists Amodeo and Wentworth have outlined a three-step process for communicating in a self-revealing and noncoercive manner.

6. Review the three-step process with the group by listing the steps on newsprint. A simple exercise as follows may be included to give group members an opportunity to experience this process. Divide the group into pairs, one of whom is designated the presenter and the other the listener. The role of the presenter is to recall a person with whom he or she is angry and to imagine the listener as that person. The listener will keep his or her head down and eyes closed in order to listen without responding. The pre-

senter then follows the three steps outlined in the chapter (identify, express, and request). Then the roles are reversed. After the exercise is complete, give the group an opportunity to reflect on the experience of the partners. Ask the presenter: "How did it feel to express anger openly?" "What other feelings were involved besides anger?" "How did it feel to express wants or expectations openly?" Ask the listener: "What did you experience as you listened to the anger of your partner?" "How did it feel to listen without responding?"

Comment: Therapist Edwin Friedman advocates that we be a nonanxious presence for each other, including nurturing playfulness and avoiding diagnosing others.

7. List Friedman's two characteristics of nonanxious presence: (a) nurturing playfulness and (b) avoiding diagnosing. Divide into cluster groups, and ask the participants to recall an experience when they or another person were a nonanxious presence. Ask: "How is being a nonanxious presence different from being passive or indifferent?" "What are some of the ways we 'diagnose' others?" "How can we nurture playfulness in relationships?"

8. In the larger group, play video segment 6B, an interview with a person who is familiar with the twelve-step program. Ask the group to listen for steps of community building.

Review the twelve-step program as outlined in the chapter. Ask the group how these steps provide insight into ways congregations can become communities of personal support. Also discuss, "How is communion a symbol for you of intimate community?"

9. Write these words of Henri Nouwen on newsprint: "The closer we come to the heart of the One who loves us with an unconditional love, the closer we come to each other in the solidarity of a redeemed humanity." In cluster groups, ask members: "How does intimacy with God lead to solidarity with others?" "What does solidarity with others mean for you?"

10. In the larger group, invite participants to share what they have learned from this course and the specific steps they can take to encourage intimacy in their personal experience between people and within their congregations.

11. Gather the group in a circle. Encourage members to express appreciation for the gift of intimacy that they may have experienced with others in the group. One-sentence prayers from participants would be an excellent ending for the course.